10.-

ENGLISH PICTURE WORDBOOK

THE ENGLISH KINDERDUDEN

Mit 27 mehrfarbigen Bildtafeln und einem
Wörterverzeichnis mit 1500 Wörtern

BIBLIOGRAPHISCHES INSTITUT · MANNHEIM/WIEN/ZÜRICH

JUGENDBUCHVERLAG

The English Kinderduden, der frei nach dem *Kinderduden* bearbeitet wurde, entstand in Gemeinschaftsarbeit der Verlage George G. Harrap & Co. Ltd, London, und Bibliographisches Institut AG, Mannheim.

First published in Great Britain 1964
by George G. Harrap & Co. Ltd
182–184 High Holborn, London WC1V 7AX

Reprinted: 1965; 1966; 1968; 1969; 1970;
1971 (twice); 1975

© *George G. Harrap & Co. Ltd, 1964*

Copyright. All rights reserved

Printed in Great Britain by Morrison & Gibb Ltd, London and Edinburgh

ISBN 3-411-00950-0

VORWORT

Der 1959 in unserem Verlag erschienene Kinderduden ist seinerzeit von Lehrern, Eltern und Schülern gleichermaßen lebhaft begrüßt worden. Nach wie vor schreiben Kinder begeisterte Briefe über dieses Buch.

Der Erfolg des deutschen Kinderdudens hat uns veranlaßt, in Gemeinschaftsarbeit mit dem Verlag George G. Harrap & Co. Ltd, London, einen englischen Kinderduden zu bearbeiten, der auf 25 Bildtafeln Szenen aus dem englischen Alltagsleben bringt.

In gleicher Art wie im deutschen Kinderduden wird mit Ziffern die Verbindung zwischen Bild und Wort hergestellt. Auch im englischen Kinderduden sind diese Wörter in kleinen Geschichten angewendet.

Alle im ersten Teil des Buches vorkommenden Wörter werden im Wörterverzeichnis, dem zweiten Teil des Buches, wiederholt. In kleinen Sätzen wird ihre Bedeutung und Anwendung gezeigt.

Bibliographisches Institut

CONTENTS

In the Sitting-room	10	At the Zoo	36
In the Bedroom	12	At the Fair	38
In the Kitchen	14	At the Sports Ground	40
In the Garden	16	At the Christmas Party	42
At the Outfitter's	18	In the Market-garden	44
In the Park	20	In the Tea-garden	46
In the Town-centre	22	On the Farm	48
At the Traffic Lights	24	In the Cow-shed	50
In the High Street	26	By the River	52
At the Market	28	At the Seaside	54
In the Grocery	30	At the New House	56
In the Classroom	32	At the Station	58
At the Hospital	34	Great Britain and Ireland	60

The United States of America . . 62

In the Sitting-room

1 Stove
2 Picture frame
3 Piano
4 Picture
5 Wireless
6 Carpet
7 Curtain
8 Reel of cotton
9 Sofa
10 Knitting needles
11 Scissors
12 Thimble
13 Needles
14 Cake
15 Postcard
16 Book
17 Pullover
18 Skirt
19 Shirt
20 Handkerchief
21 Television
22 Knot
23 Button
24 Bunch of flowers
25 Vase
26 Sleeve
27 Toy cupboard
28 Cupboard curtains
29 Tear (*i.e.*, the sleeve is torn)
30 Wallpaper
31 Model aircraft
32 Toys
33 Shelf
34 Chair

July 14th was Mary's birthday. She was ten years old. Her mother suggested that she should give a small party, and she made a lovely birthday cake for Mary and put ten candles on it.

When Mary's friends arrived everything was ready in the sitting-room. They all decided that they would like to play some games before tea. They began with "Blind Man's Buff," and Mary blindfolded her friend Jimmy with a large white handkerchief.

"I can't see a thing," complained Jimmy.

"You're not supposed to," said Mary, and turned him round three times.

Jimmy staggered round the room and at last caught hold of John.

"Look, you've torn my sleeve," cried John.

"I'm terribly sorry," said Jimmy. "I didn't mean to."

After tea the children all wanted to play "Hunt the Thimble." Everyone went out of the room while Rosemary, one of the guests, hid the thimble. She put it under the wireless on the piano.

1
2
3
4
5
6
7
8
9
10
11
12
13
14
15
16
17
18
19
20
21
22
23
24
25
26
27
28
29
30
31
32
33
34

In the Bedroom

1 Wardrobe
2 Hand-towel
3 Mirror
4 Shower
5 Soap
6 Face flannel
7 Wash-hand basin
8 Bath
9 Bath mat
10 Alarm clock
11 Stockings
12 Comb
13 Hair
14 Switch
15 Pyjamas
16 Jacket
17 Trousers
18 Belt
19 Socks
20 Moon
21 Bedstead
22 Bedspread
23 Pillow
24 Lamp
25 Rug
26 Teddy-bear
27 Doll
28 Night-gown
29 Slipper
30 Bedside table
31 Door

Every night Mary goes to say good-night to John. She always takes her dolls with her.

"I don't want to see your silly dolls," says John.

"They're sweet," replies Mary. "And anyway, you used to have a teddy-bear."

Mrs Brown likes the children to be in bed by eight o'clock. They have to be up early in the morning for school. John does not like getting up, so he has to have an alarm clock. He also does not like going to bed. Mrs Brown always asks the children if they have washed their faces and cleaned their teeth, because they sometimes forget.

As John is older than Mary he is allowed to read in bed. He therefore has a bedside lamp. Sometimes the moon shines through his bedroom window and he can read without his mother knowing.

Mary's bedroom is always very tidy, but John is an untidy boy. His mother makes him fold his clothes and put them on a chair ready for the morning.

Mary sleeps in a room next door to John's: When Mrs Brown has gone downstairs Mary often creeps into John's room because she likes him to read stories to her. If Mrs Brown knew about this she would be very annoyed.

1
2
3
4
5
6
7
8
9
10
11
12
13
14
15
16
17
18
19
20
21
22
23
24
25
26
27
28
29
30
31

In the Kitchen

1 Saucepan
2 Stewed fruit
3 Frying-pan
4 Jelly
5 Glasses
6 Bowl
7 Custard
8 Lid
9 Jam
10 Electric mixer
11 Mother
12 Pastry
13 Herring (a fish)
14 Cat
15 Ham
16 Father
17 Soup
18 Stove
19 Coke
20 Jug
21 Colander
22 Funnel

On Sundays John and Mary help their mother to prepare the lunch. Yesterday Mrs Brown bought a leg of lamb, which she is now going to cook. While she is peeling the potatoes the children like to make pastry. John likes cutting the pastry into different shapes and putting the jam into the pies. Mary rolls out the pastry.

"Put the cat out into the garden, John," said Mrs Brown. "He's getting under my feet. And would you ask Daddy to bring some coke in for the stove, please?"

Mary put the pastry boards away and started to make a cake. To the flour she added some eggs and milk and a pinch of salt.

"Shall I beat the Yorkshire Pudding in the electric mixer?" she asked her mother.

"Yes, I should," replied Mrs Brown. "It's getting late and we must have lunch on time. Daddy wants to play golf this afternoon."

Soon everything was ready, and the table had been laid in the dining-room.

"Call your father, dear," said Mrs Brown to Mary. "It's all ready now."

Mr Brown came in and lifted the leg of lamb out of the cooker.

"The lunch smells good," he said. "I feel hungry after my morning's work in the garden."

After the family had finished lunch the children washed the dishes, Mrs Brown read the Sunday papers, and Mr Brown went out to play golf.

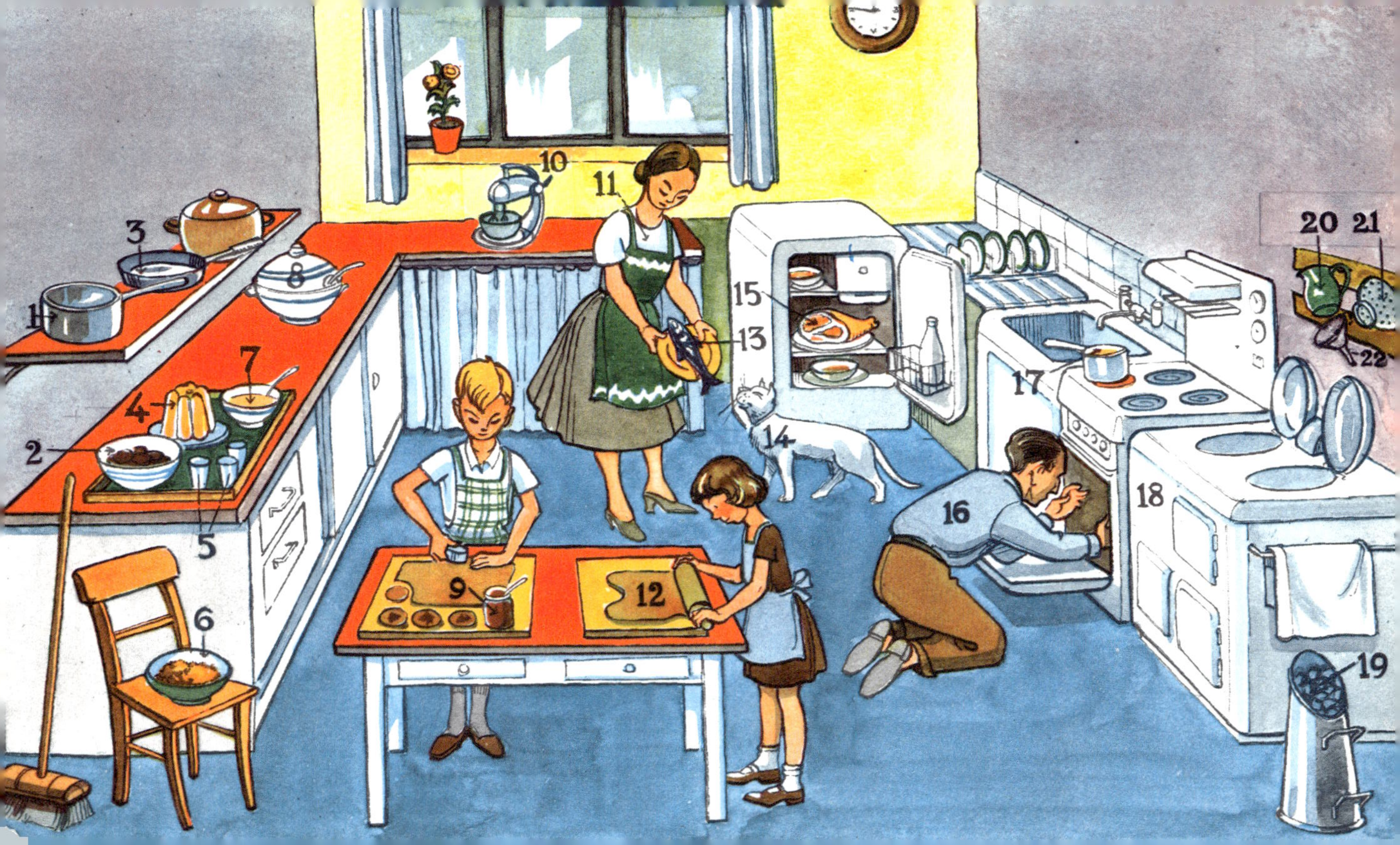
1
2
3
4
5
6
7
8
9
10
11
12
13
14
15
16
17
18
19
20
21
22

In the Garden

1 Grass
2 Tap
3 Hose
4 Fruit tree
5 Blossom
6 Fence
7 Earth (vegetable plot)
8 Worm
9 Toad
10 Hedgehog
11 Garden gate
12 Frog
13 Nest
14 Branch
15 Butterfly
16 Beetle
17 Leaf
18 Caterpillar
19 Snail
20 Rabbit
21 Neighbour
22 Tulip
23 Stem
24 Swing
25 Bush, shrub

Mr Brown is a keen gardener. When the weather is fine Mrs Brown and the children help him to mow the lawn.

Mary loves picking flowers. In the Spring the garden is full of many different flowers. She likes to arrange some in a bowl for her bedroom.

John is not interested in gardening. He likes collecting snails, caterpillars, and worms. In fact his favourite subject at school is Biology.

There is a rabbit-hutch overlooking the Browns' garden. It belongs to their next-door neighbours. When his father is not looking John stands on the flower-bed and pushes lettuce through the door of the hutch. He always longs to climb over the fence and see the rabbits more closely.

One afternoon, when the Brown family was busy in the garden, the boy next door was on the swing.

"I can see you!" he called to John and Mary.
"Who's that?" asked John.
"The boy next door," replied Mary. "He's going so high that he can see into our garden."
The boy got off his swing and came over to the fence.
"Would you like to come and see my rabbits?" he asked.

John ran over to him. "Oh, yes please," he said. "That's what I've wanted to do for weeks. May I come round now?"
"Yes, come on," shouted the boy. John was delighted and rushed next door.

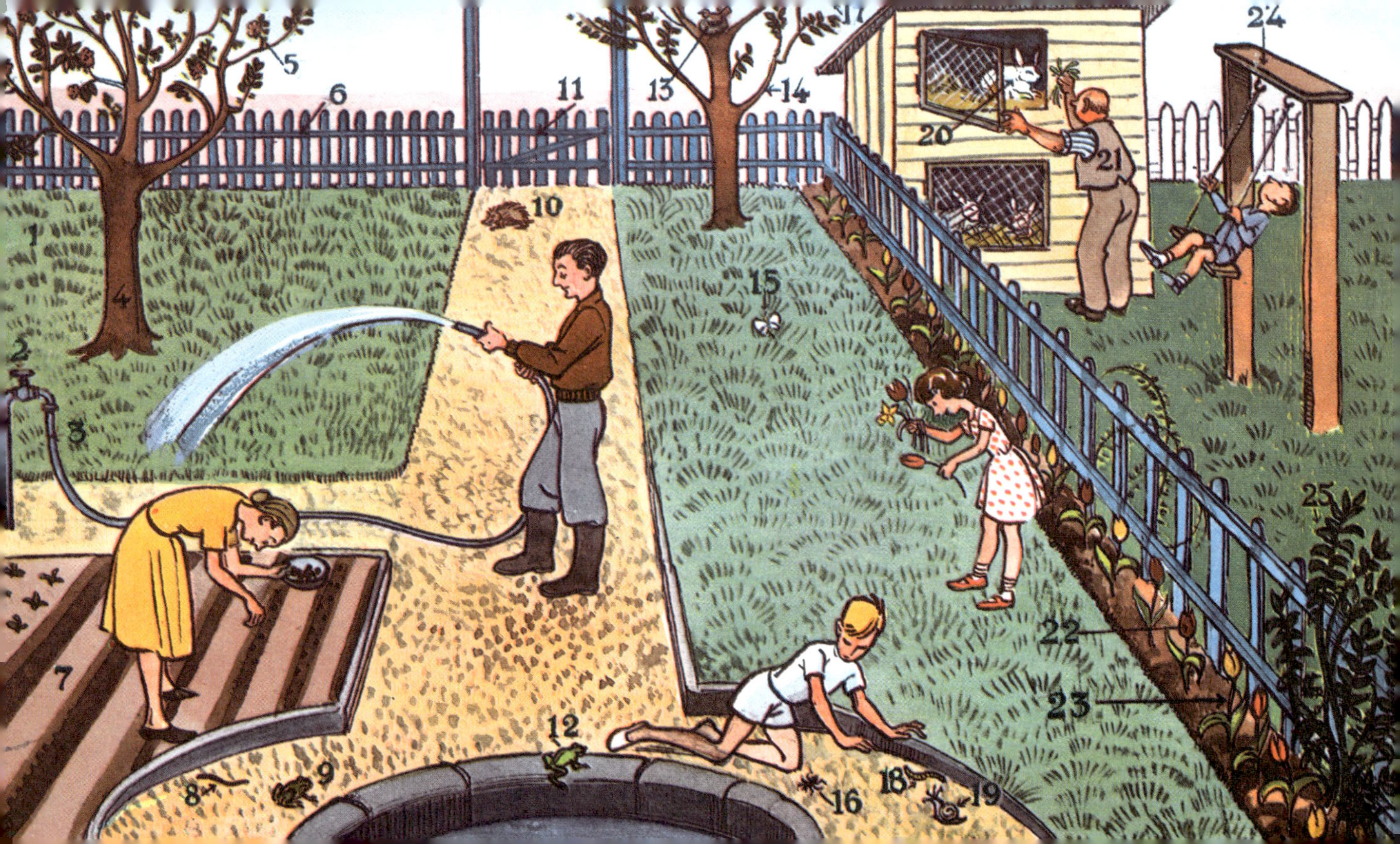
1
2
3
4
5
6
7
8
9
10
11
12
13
14
15
16
17
18
19
20
21
22
23
24
25

At the Outfitter's

1 Skis
2 Boxing-gloves
3 Golf clubs
4 Golf bag
5 Cricket stumps
6 Cricket bat
7 Cricket ball
8 Gum boots
9 Sun glasses
10 Tennis dress
11 Felt hat
12 Gloves
13 Table-tennis bat
14 Vest
15 Raincoat
16 Hockey stick
17 Shirt
18 Shorts
19 Blazer
20 Sweater
21 Shop assistant
22 Wrist
23 Scarf
24 Tennis racquet
25 Tennis balls
26 Thigh
27 Calf of leg
28 Partition
29 Lips
30 Reflection

As the holidays were nearly over, Mrs Brown took John and Mary to the school outfitter's as they needed some new clothes. On the way they met Aunt Jean and their two cousins, who were going to buy some shoes.

When they entered the shop an assistant came over to them.

"Good morning," said Mrs Brown. "I want to buy a new blazer for Mary and also a new school cap for John."

The assistant took Mary's size, and while Mary tried on the blazer John looked at some sun glasses.

"This blazer seems to fit very well, madam," said the assistant.

"Good," said Mrs Brown, "then we shall buy it. Do you like it, Mary?"

"It is lovely," said Mary, who was thrilled with the blazer.

While the assistant parcelled up the blazer, Mrs Brown chose a cap for John.

As Aunt Jean had already bought new shoes for the cousins she all helped John to choose a cricket bat.

At last it was time for them to go. The children were sorry that they could not buy more new clothes.

SPORTS

FOOTWEAR

SHIRTS - UNDERWEAR - SOCKS - GLOVES - TIES

In the Park

1 Hedge
2 Bush
3 Pond
4 Brook
5 Bulrushes
6 Swan
7 Shawl
8 Dog's lead
9 Dachshund
10 Bread
11 Ice-cream
12 Ice-cream man
13 Newspaper
14 Tie
15 Seat
16 Chestnut tree
17 Chute
18 Wheelbarrow
19 Fir tree
20 Playground
21 Fist
22 Pigtail
23 Stream

The Browns' house is not far away from the large park in the centre of the town. Mary and John often walk in the park on Saturday afternoons.

They take some bread with them because they like to feed the swans on the pond. Mary is a little afraid of them because they sound so fierce when they hiss at one another.

There is often a man selling ice-cream near the pond.

"I should love a sixpenny cornet," says Mary every time she sees him.

John has not time to eat ice-cream as he is so busy feeding the swans.

There are always many other people in the park when Mary and John are there. There is an old lady who takes her dog for a walk every Saturday afternoon, and a gentleman who sits and reads his newspapers on one of the park benches. There are also several children who go to play games in the park. Nearly all the children love sliding down the chute.

"Come on, Mary," says John. "Let's go for a slide." John slides down the chute at great speed. "Oh, it's marvellous!" he cries. Mary, however, prefers to watch the others and not to slide down the chute herself.

Before the children leave the park, John always goes to talk to one of the gardeners. Sometimes, if he is lucky, the gardener gives him some snails or caterpillars.

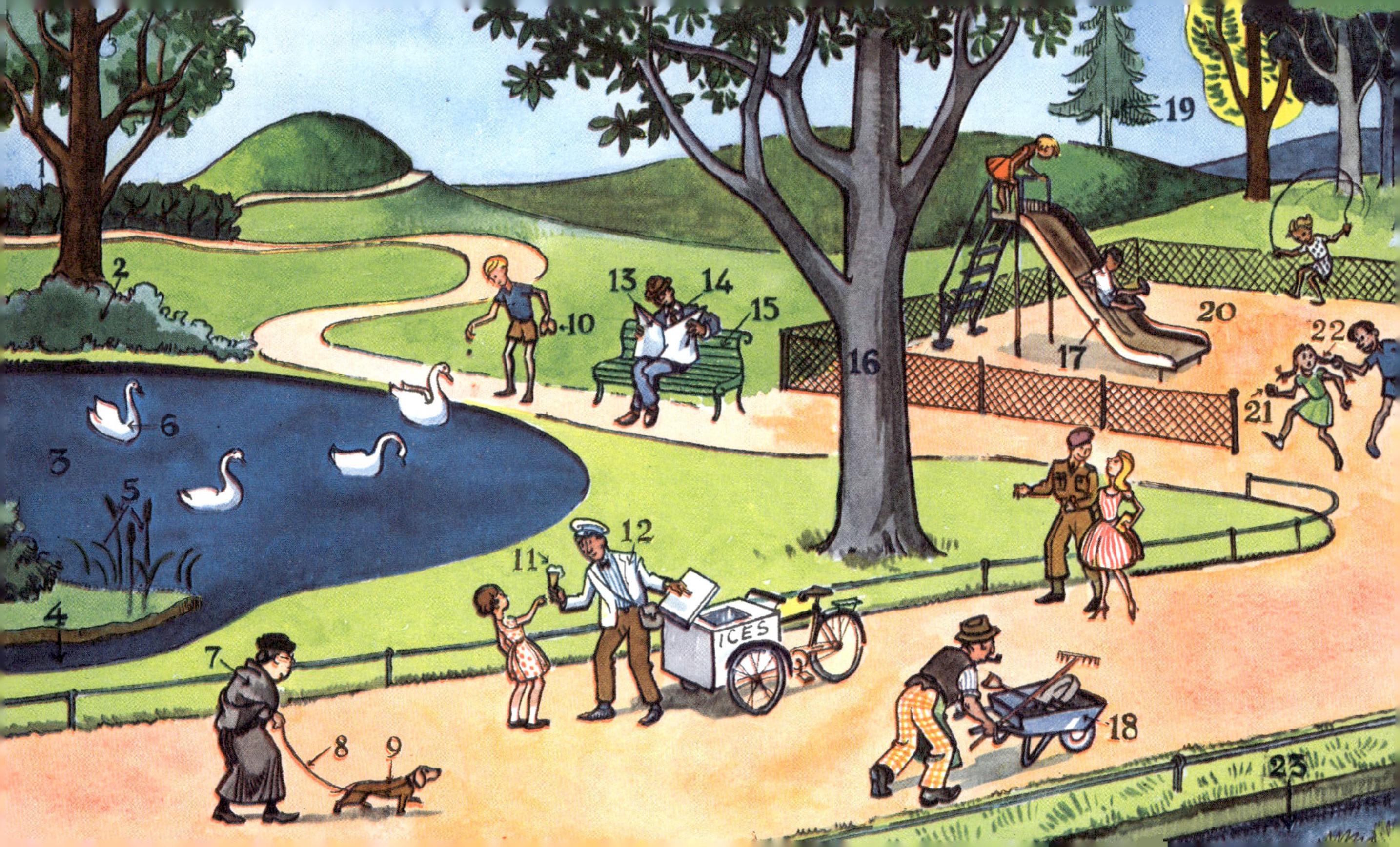
1
2
3
4
5
6
7
8
9
10
11
12
13
14
15
16
17
18
19
20
21
22
23
ICES

In the Town-centre

1 Chemist's shop
2 Chemist
3 Police station
4 Bracket (lamp)
5 Lamp
6 Post Office
7 Steps
8 Workman
9 Spire
10 Town Hall
11 Post box
12 Letter
13 Stamp
14 Steam-roller
15 Asphalt
16 Balcony
17 Clock
18 House
19 Door
20 Fountain
21 Cinema
22 Poster
23 Coloured man
24 Paste
25 Butcher's shop
26 Beam
27 Craftsman
28 Pincers
29 Nail

On Saturday mornings Mrs Brown sends John and Mary out to do the shopping. She gives them the shopping-list, a large basket, and some money in a purse.

"Don't lose the change," she says to them.

The children can buy all their mother needs in the town-centre nearby. There is a fountain near the cinema, and Mary always stops to look at it.

One Saturday there was a steam-roller in the street.

"Look, they're mending the road," said John. "I should love to have a ride on the steam-roller."

"Come on," said Mary. "We've lots to do.

You go to the chemist's and buy Mummy some soap. And would you post this letter on the way?"

Mary then went to the butcher's shop.

"Good morning," said the butcher. "What a lovely day it is."

"Hello, Mr Dawson," replied Mary. "I've come for our usual Sunday leg of lamb."

In the meantime John had bought the soap and posted the letter. Then he went to see what films were on at the cinema.

A man was sticking a poster on the wall. It was a picture of a coloured man, and the film was about Africa. Mary and John wanted to see the picture.

CHEMIST
POLICE
POST OFFICE
CINEMA
CINEMA
BUTCHER
TOYS AND
1
2
3
4
5
6
7
8
9
10
11
12
13
14
15
16
17
18
19
20
21
22
23
24
25
26
27
28
29

At the Traffic Lights

1. Belisha beacon
2. Pedestrian crossing
3. Tanker
4. Lorry
5. Coal sack
6. Garage
7. Van
8. Tyre
9. Mudguard
10. Coalman
11. Traffic lights
12. Policeman
13. Cyclist
14. Cycle
15. Car
16. School bag
17. Petrol pump
18. Motor coach
19. Windscreen
20. Steering-wheel
21. Motor cycle
22. Scooter
23. Boot
24. Inn sign
25. Pillar-box
26. Bumper

One day after lunch, Mary and John were walking back to school down the High Street, when they saw their uncle's car. It had stopped at the traffic lights.

"If we run," said John, "we'll manage to get into the car before the lights change."

The lights were still red when the children reached the car.

"Get in quickly," said their uncle.

"Yes, hurry," said their two cousins, who were in the back of the car. But it was not easy for the children to open the car door in a hurry.

Suddenly a policeman came up and stood in front of the car.

"Do you realize, sir, that you are holding up all the traffic?" he said in a loud voice.

Uncle George looked at the lights and saw that they were green.

"I'm very sorry indeed," he replied. "I was waiting for the children to get into the car safely."

"You should know that you must never park at traffic lights," said the policeman gruffly. "It is a serious offence, and if I see you parking here again I shall have to report you."

"I do apologize," replied Uncle George.

When the lights had turned green again they drove quickly away through the town.

GARAGE
REPAIRS
ACCESSORIES - SPARES
CROWN SERVICE
CROWN HOTEL
OIL
Smiths Tours
COOPER'S COALS
1
2
3
4
5
6
7
8
9
10
11
12
13
14
15
16
17
18
19
20
21
22
23
24
25
26

In the High Street

1 Sun-blind
2 Chocolates
3 Mother
4 Sweets
5 Shopping-basket
6 Loaf
7 Rolls
8 Baker
9 Assistant
10 Uniform
11 Wall
12 Leather
13 Bootmaker
14 Stool
15 Boots
16 Shoes
17 Sweep
18 Painter
19 Tailor
20 Carpenter
21 Hammer
22 Plank
23 Locksmith
24 Key
25 Entrance
26 Glazier
27 Pane of glass

Mrs Brown does most of her shopping in the High Street. All the main shops are in this street.

There is a sweet-shop, where Mrs Brown always buys a big box of chocolates for John and Mary. Next door to the sweet-shop is a large bakery. This shop sells fresh, home-made bread. This is the Brown family's favourite bread.

John is having a new pair of long trousers for his thirteenth birthday. His mother is buying them at the tailor's in the High Street. It is a very large shop with two work-rooms above it. John and his mother will not have to spend much time at the tailor's as Mrs Brown already knows his size.

Mary had holes in the soles of a pair of her shoes. Mrs Brown, therefore, took them to the bootmaker's.

"These shoes have worn badly," said the bootmaker. "I shall have to put new soles on both of them."

"When will they be ready?" asked Mrs Brown.

"In about a week's time," he replied.

Mrs Brown noticed the sweep's van out of the bootmaker's window.

"I must ask Mr Smith to come and sweep our chimneys," she said.

Mrs Brown also saw the local carpenter crossing the road, carrying a large plank of wood. She wanted the carpenter to put some new hinges on her kitchen door.

1869
Chocolates
BAKER
CONFECTIONER
BOOTMAKER
TAILOR
SWEEP
1
2
3
4
5
6
7
8
9
10
11
12
13
14
15
16
17
18
19
20
21
22
23
24
25
26
27

At the Market

1 Stall-holder
2 Gooseberries
3 Grapes
4 Cherries
5 Parsley
6 Apricots
7 Raspberries
8 Red currants
9 Stall
10 Peaches
11 Strawberries
12 Tomatoes
13 Potatoes
14 Housewife
15 Narcissi
16 Marguerites
17 Carnations
18 Lily of the Valley
19 Iris
20 Daffodils
21 Roses
22 Violets
23 Lilac

John and Mary love market day. They spend the whole morning looking at all the different stalls. They also do some shopping for their mother.

Their favourite stall in the market is the greengrocer's stall. The flowers and vegetables are so colourful, and there is always a lovely fresh smell. There are so many flowers and so much fruit that it is difficult to choose which sort to buy.

There are shiny red apples, juicy peaches, home-grown tomatoes, big bunches of grapes and bananas, and many other different kinds of fruit.

John loves cherries and he could see great bunches of them on the stall opposite.

"Look at those cherries, Mary," he exclaimed. "Don't they look delicious!"

"Buy some to take home," replied Mary, "but don't eat them all here."

Mary was buying some flowers to take home for her mother. Unfortunately she could not afford to buy them all, but she decided to buy some carnations.

"That will be thirty pence," said the lady behind the counter. Mary gave her the money and put the flowers in her basket. She had some money left over, so she decided to buy some violets for her grandmother.

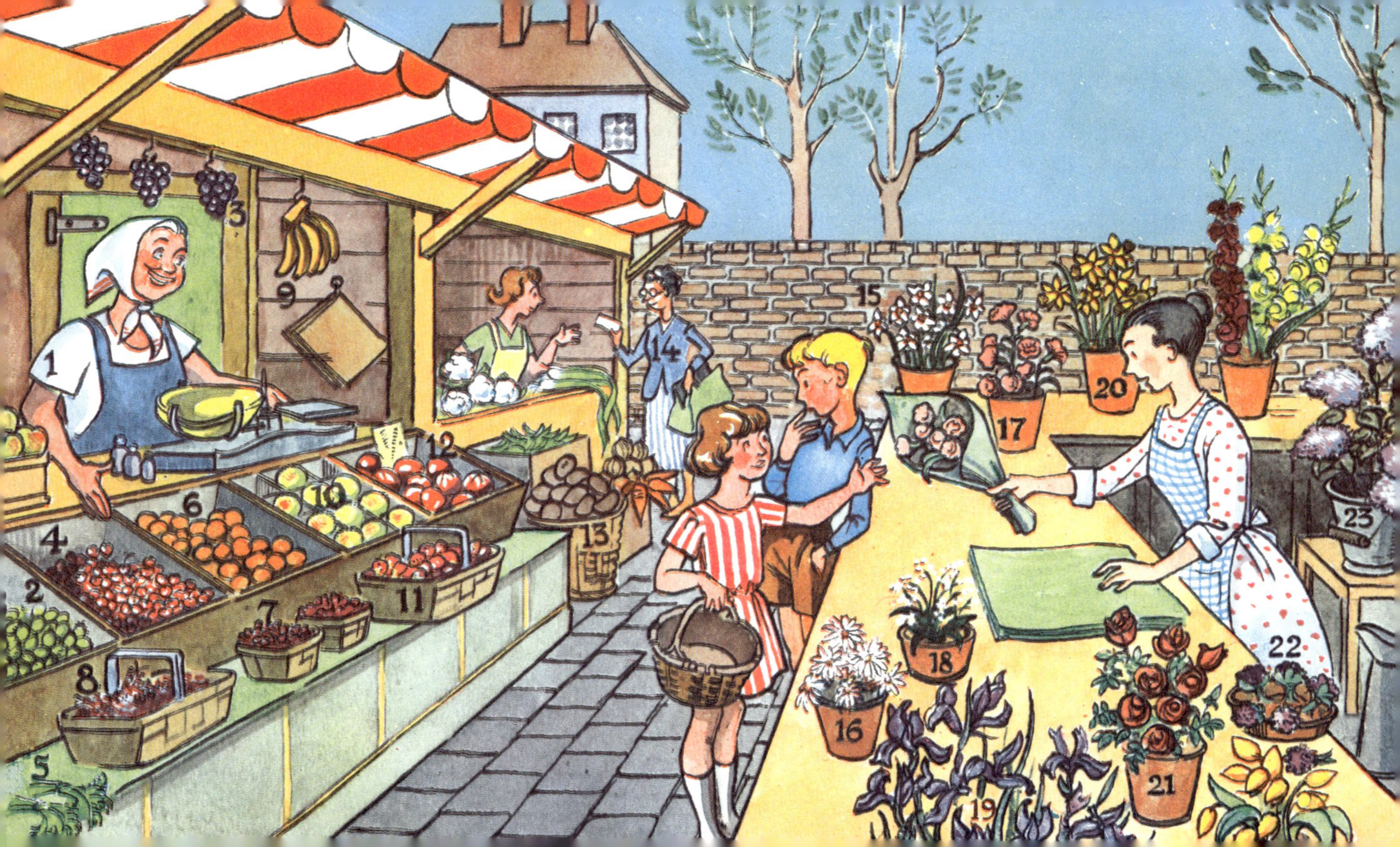

1
2
3
4
5
6
7
8
9
10
11
12
13
14
15
16
17
18
19
20
21
22
23

In the Grocery

1 Cinnamon
2 Sugar
3 Rice
4 Rope
5 Vanilla
6 Salt
7 Butter
8 Sack
9 Pepper
10 Grocer
11 Scales
12 String
13 Cheese
14 Eggs
15 Nuts
16 Onions
17 Beans
18 Shop door
19 Coin
20 Bananas
21 Box
22 Cash register
23 Carton
24 Oranges
25 Oil
26 Vinegar
27 Lard
28 Weights
29 Bags
30 Lemons

Mary and John like to go shopping with their mother. Mrs Brown buys her groceries from the grocer's shop in the High Street. The shop is often busy.

One day a stout gentleman came into the shop smoking a pipe.

"I think he is a salesman," said John.

"How do you know?" asked Mary.

"Because salesmen often carry brief-cases," replied John.

At that moment an old lady dropped some money on the floor. Mary stooped to pick it up.

"Thank you, my dear," said the old lady. "I'm getting too old to bend down as far as that."

At last it was Mrs Brown's turn. She had a long shopping list with her, and as she read the items out the grocer put them into her bag.

"I think that is all for to-day," said Mrs Brown. "How much is that?"

"Mummy, you have forgotten the flour," interrupted Mary. "I am going to make some cakes this afternoon, and there is none left."

"Thank you for reminding me, Mary," said Mrs Brown.

So they bought the flour and paid for all Mrs Brown's groceries.

VINEGAR
PEPPER
VANILLA
SALT
SPICE
1
2
3
4
5
6
7
8
9
10
11
12
13
14
15
16
17
18
19
20
21
22
23
24
25
26
27
28
29
30

In the Classroom

1 Classroom
2 Blackboard
3 Duster
4 Chalk
5 Register
6 Desk
7 Ruler
8 Waste-paper basket
9 Teacher
10 Pen
11 Ink
12 India rubber
13 Pencil
14 Exercise book
15 School bag
16 Pupil
17 Map
18 Timetable
19 Forefinger

School starts at nine o'clock. Mary is always punctual, but John is often late. Mr Grant, the teacher, gets very angry with him. John tries to creep into the classroom unseen, but the teacher always sees him.

"You're late, John!" shouts Mr Grant. "If it happens again there will be serious trouble. What is your excuse to-day?"

"I'm sorry, sir," says John. "I forgot my history book, so I had to go back home."

"Well, you must go and stand at the back of the class," says the teacher.

The register has already been called. The teacher has written on the blackboard and the class is ready for the first lesson. John does not like school. While Mr Grant is talking he looks at the map of the British Isles on the wall.

"I wish you would concentrate," complains the teacher. "You will never pass your exams at the end of term."

Some of the children in John's class are very clever. They know the answers to all the teacher's questions. One girl puts her hand up every time he asks a question.

Mr Grant is very strict. He likes the classroom to be tidy. No one is allowed to have an untidy desk.

John's exercise books are full of ink-blots. This also makes the teacher very cross. John does not think that lessons are important. He wants to be a farmer.

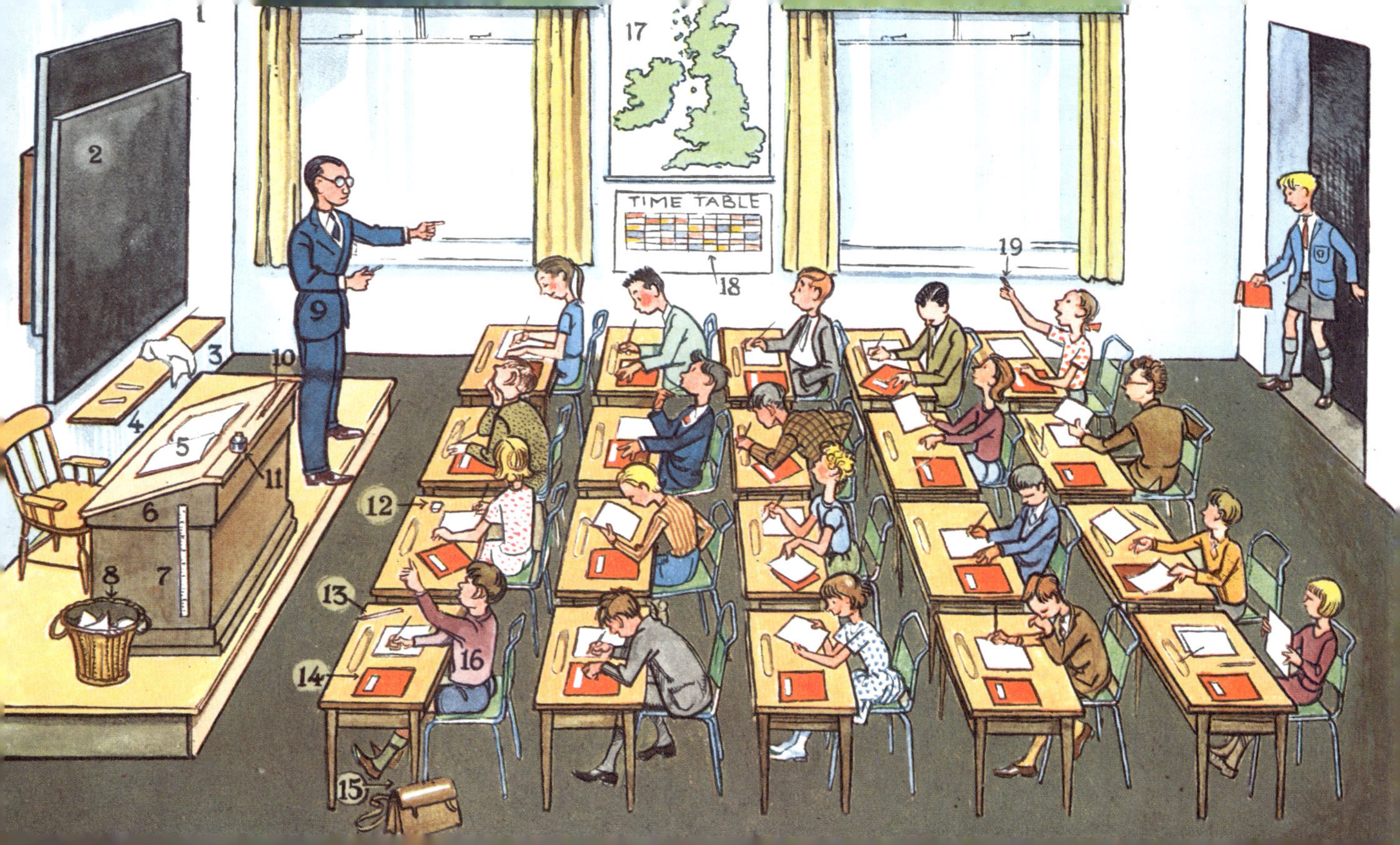

TIME TABLE
1
2
3
4
5
6
7
8
9
10
11
12
13
14
15
16
17
18
19

At the Hospital

1 Surgery
2 Patient
3 Head
4 Blood
5 Thumb
6 Syringe
7 Nurse
8 Telephone
9 Waiting-room
10 Ear
11 Tooth
12 Elbow
13 Thermometer
14 Forehead
15 Tongue
16 Neck
17 Stomach
18 Medicine
19 Bandage
20 Nose
21 Plaster
22 Mouth
23 Ointment
24 Face
25 Wound
26 Knee
27 Boil
28 Cheek

One day in the playground at school Mary fell and cut her knee. The cut was very deep, so John was asked to take Mary home. When Mrs Brown had seen the cut she decided to take Mary to the hospital. Mary was very frightened. "There's nothing to be afraid of," said her mother. "The nurses won't hurt you."

At the hospital Mary and Mrs Brown were taken to the Casualty Department.

"Come this way," said a kind nurse. "I'll look after you."

There were several other children waiting to be treated. One boy had a bandage round his head.

Mary sat on a chair and held her leg up for the nurse to see.

"I don't think you will need stitches in your knee," she said, "so I'll clean the cut and then put a dressing on it."

In the meantime, John had wandered off. He noticed that a man on a stretcher-trolley had been taken into the room next door. He wondered what was wrong with him. The man's face was very pale.

The nurse was so kind and gentle that Mary was soon no longer afraid.

"This will take some time to heal," said the nurse, "so I think you had better stay in bed for a couple of days."

"Lucky thing," said John. "You won't have to go to school."

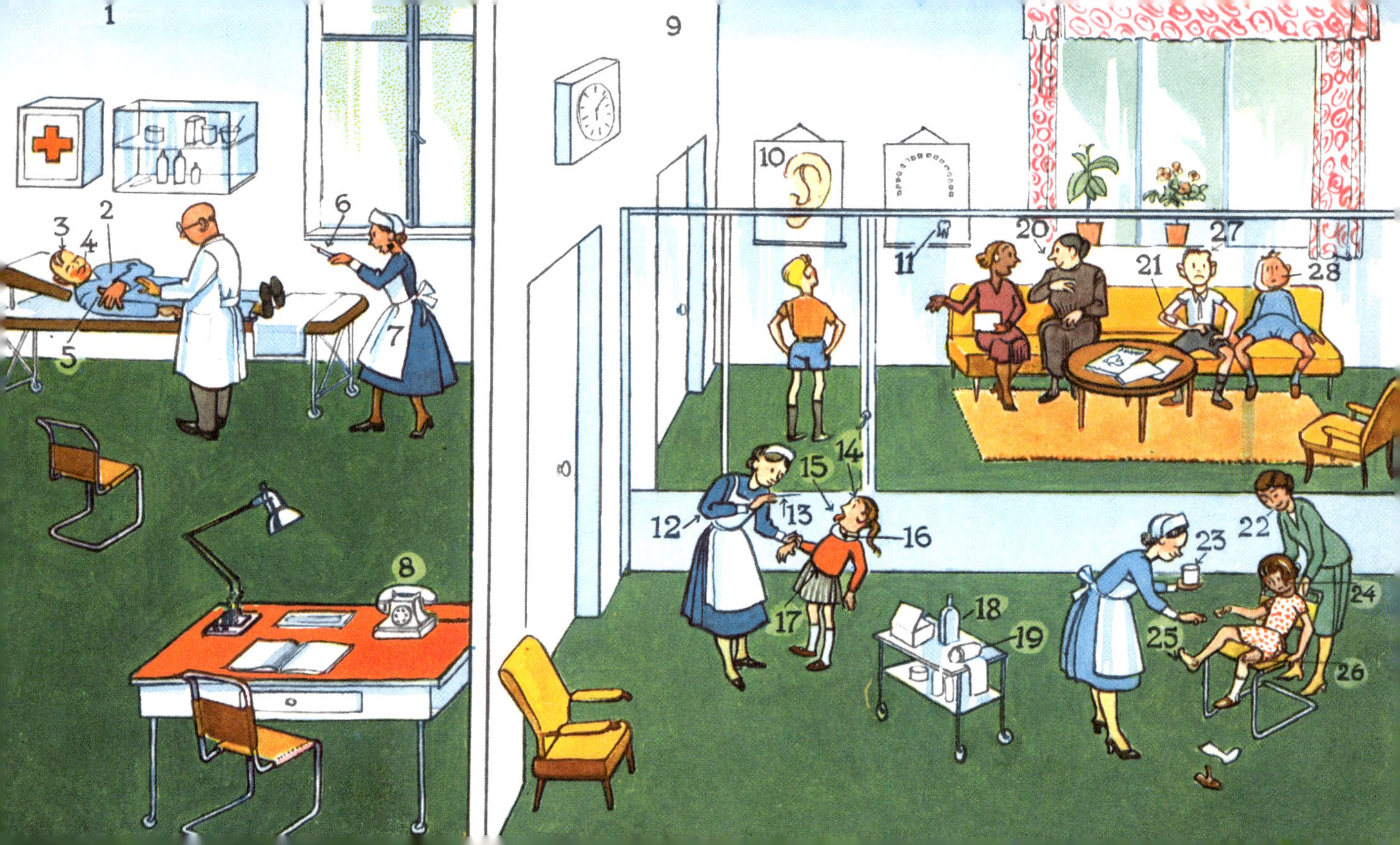
1
2
3
4
5
6
7
8
9
10
11
12
13
14
15
16
17
18
19
20
21
22
23
24
25
26
27
28

At the Zoo

1 Hippopotamus
2 Pony
3 Rhinoceros
4 Giraffe
5 Brown bear
6 Monkey
7 Zebra
8 Keeper
9 Kangaroo
10 Tiger
11 Paw
12 Cage
13 Leopard
14 Lion
15 Polar bear

One of Mary and John's favourite outings is a visit to the zoo. John is especially fond of animals. Mary also likes looking at them. She likes the baby animals and the monkeys best.

The zoo near the Browns' home is not very large. There are, however, many animals that Mary and John would not normally see.

John likes to take some bread with him so that he can feed the animals. He also sometimes takes some fish so that he can feed the polar bears.

"Watch, Mary," he says excitedly, "how the bears catch the fish in mid-air."

Mary is not really interested. While John stands and watches the bears eating his fish she goes off and has a ride in the pony cart.

There is a tame bear at the zoo. Mary loves to watch it doing its tricks.

Sometimes Mary and John arrive in time to watch all the animals being fed by the keepers. John is fascinated by the lions. He is also a little frightened of them because they are so big and they roar so loudly.

"Look how much they eat," he exclaims.

"That's as much as our dog eats in a month!"

"Don't stand so close," says Mary. "They might eat you too."

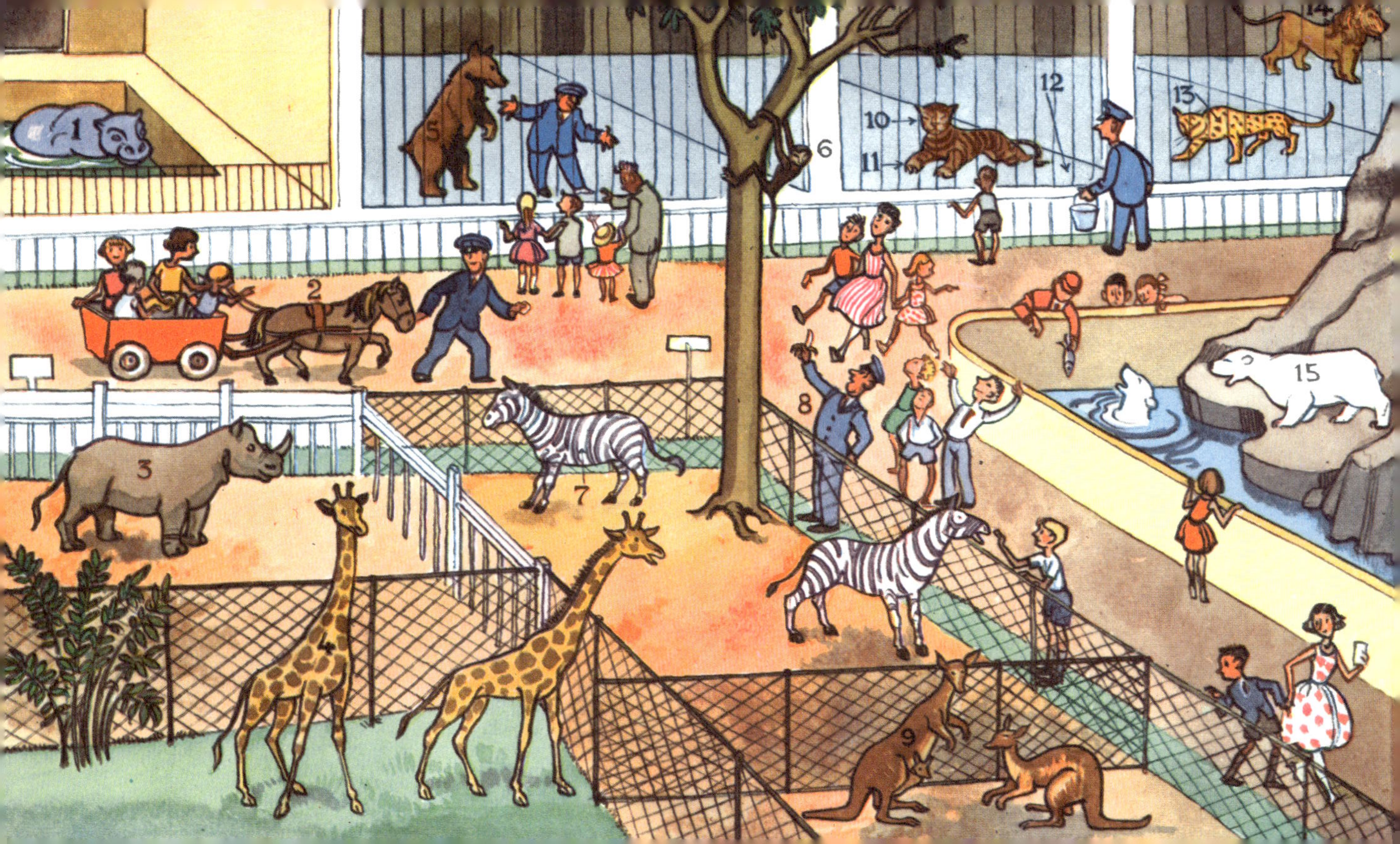
1
2
3
4
5
6
7
8
9
10
11
12
13
14
15

At the Fair

1 Circus
2 Rifle range
3 Air-gun
4 Spectator
5 Bear
6 Chain
7 Scooter
8 Clown
9 Camel
10 Fairground
11 Red Indian
12 Roundabout (or Merry-go-round)
13 Coconut-shy
14 Elephant
15 Pole
16 Balloon
17 Flag
18 Dodgem cars
19 Donkey
20 Uncle
21 Punch and Judy show
22 Punch

Mary and John are always very excited when the circus comes to town. Mr Brown buys tickets for them to see the show in the big tent. They always spend a long time in the fairground. There is so much to see and so much noise. There are always dodgem cars, which John loves to drive. John loves the roundabout. But Mary does not because it makes her feel sick. She likes watching the Punch and Judy show. She also likes to have a ride on the donkey.

John spends nearly all his pocket-money at the Rifle Range.

"Don't waste all your money," says Mary. "You won't have any left to buy an ice-cream in the big tent."

"Be quiet," replies John. "Now I've missed the target again."

John always has a turn on the Coconut-shy, but he has never managed to win a coconut.

There is usually a lady selling balloons.

The fairground is so fascinating that they almost miss the circus in the big tent.

"Hurry up," Mary calls to John. "We'll never find our seats."

"The last show hasn't finished yet," he replies. "We still have plenty of time."

But Mary is right. At the last minute she can never find John. They only just manage to sit down before the show begins.

38

GRAND CIRCUS
1
2
RIFLE RANGE
3
5
6
7
8
9
10
11
12
13
14
15
16
17
18
19
20
21
22
DODGEM CARS
PAY HERE
PUNCH AND JUDY

At the Sports Ground

1. Tape
2. Track
3. Sand-heap
4. Shovel
5. Track-suit
6. Sand-pit
7. Jumper
8. Competitors
9. Eye
10. Chest
11. Hand
12. Shin
13. Foot
14. Shoulder
15. Friend
16. Cross-bar
17. Goal
18. Goalkeeper
19. Football ground
20. Ball
21. Players
22. Back
23. Running shoe
24. The number

At school John and Mary both like to play games. The boys have races to see who can run the fastest and often John wins. John's favourite game is football.

One day John fell and hurt himself while he was playing football, so his friend Peter took him to a seat where he rested for a while.

"Does your knee hurt, John?" asked the games master. "Perhaps I had better call Doctor Archer."

"I am sure it will be better soon," replied John.

The master examined his knee and rubbed it gently.

"That feels fine," said John, standing up. "Can I play football again now?"

"I think it would be better if you rested your leg to-day, and then you will be fit to play in the match to-morrow," said the master.

John was very pleased that he had been chosen to play in the match. He hoped that he would score a goal for his team, but he knew that the competitors were very good too.

Mary likes the long-jump best of all. She runs quickly up to the jump, and then throws herself onto the sand. The distance which she jumps is measured with a tape.

"Well done, Mary!" cry her friends when they see that she has jumped farther than them all.

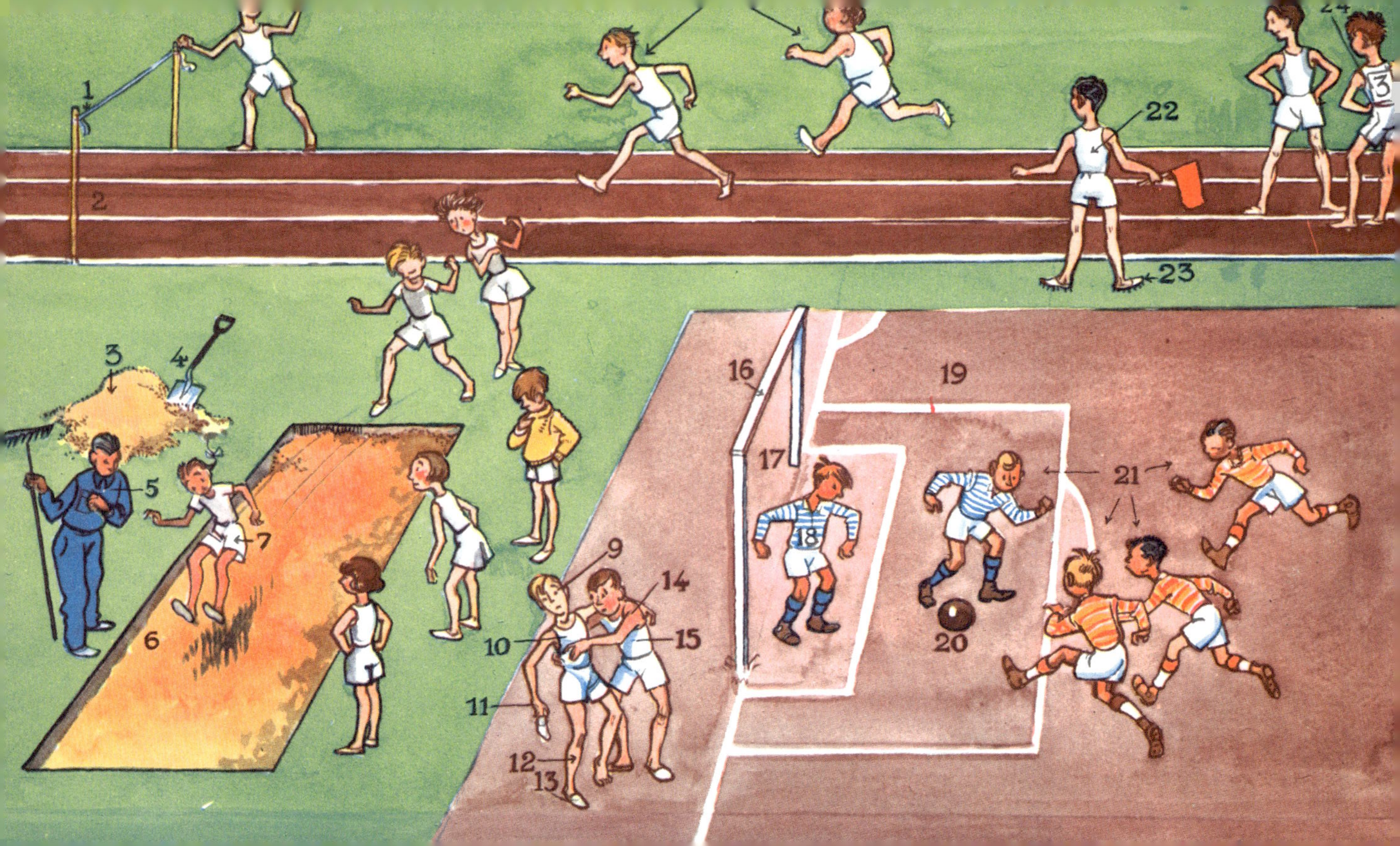
1
2
3
4
5
6
7
9
10
11
12
13
14
15
16
17
18
19
20
21
22
23
3

At the Christmas Party

1 Wall
2 Pelmet
3 Skirting board
4 Floor
5 Balloon
6 Carol-singers
7 Snow
8 Jelly
9 Mince pies
10 Crate
11 Sausage rolls
12 Blancmange
13 Sandwiches
14 Siphon
15 Milk bottle
16 Paper hat
17 Trumpet
18 Wrapping-paper
19 Pineapple
20 Lemonade
21 Trifle
22 Custard
23 Crackers
24 Christmas pudding
25 Present
26 String
27 Meringues
28 Paper chain
29 Father Christmas
30 Candle
31 Christmas tree
32 Tub
33 Rifle
34 Hearth rug
35 Holly
36 Christmas card
37 Mantelpiece
38 Fireplace
39 Grate
40 Hearth
41 Fender
42 Doll's pram

On Christmas Day John and Mary had a party and they invited all their friends. Mrs Brown made some lovely food for the party, and there was a Christmas pudding with holly on it.

"Let's pull the crackers now," said John, "so that we can wear our paper hats at tea."

After tea Mr Brown dressed up as Father Christmas, and gave all the children a present from the Christmas tree which John and Mary had decorated a few days before. They quickly unwrapped their parcels.

"Look," cried Mary, "Father Christmas has brought me a lovely baby doll."

John was very pleased too, as his present was a toy rifle.

Suddenly there was the sound of singing outside the window.

"Open the curtains," said Mrs Brown. "It must be the carol-singers."

When they had sung two carols Mrs Brown invited the carol-singers in for some food and a hot drink as it was snowing outside and they were all very cold.

1
3
4
5
6
7
8
9
10
11
12
13
14
15
16
17
18
19
20
21
22
23
24
25
26
27
28
29
30
31
32
33
34
36
37
38
39
40
41
42

In the Market-garden

1. Greenhouse
2. Gardener
3. Watering-can
4. Runner beans
5. Soil
6. Spade
7. Rake
8. Hoe
9. Radishes
10. Red-currant bushes
11. Plants
12. Hand-truck
13. Carrots
14. Stone (fruit-stone)
15. Pear
16. Apple
17. Lettuce
18. Stall
19. Flower-pot
20. Saleswoman
21. Red cabbage
22. Basket
23. Vegetable marrow
24. Cucumber
25. Cauliflower
26. Cabbage

John and Mary always go to see their uncle and aunt during the summer holidays. They have a house with a big garden twenty miles from London. Uncle Richard is very kind and often lets them pick the flowers and the fruit. In return the children help to hoe the vegetable beds.

To-day is the 28th July. It is a hot sunny day. Mary is wearing a thin cotton dress and John is wearing shorts and an open shirt. John is picking the cherries, and his uncle will sell them. John is eating one of them and spits out the stone.

"Oh, you are rude!" says Mary.

"Be quiet," says John, "I've seen you do it yourself."

Mary is more interested in the flowers. She is going to pick a bunch of them to take home for her mother. If she is lucky Uncle Richard will also let her pick some of the tomatoes in the greenhouse.

When Uncle has finished watering his young plants he will be ready to lunch with John and Mary. Aunt Susan has a surprise for the children. She has provided for each of them their favourite lunch. There will be cold meat with lettuce, tomato, and cucumber for John, and hot roast lamb with cauliflower and red-currant jelly for Mary. After that John will have apple-pie and nice fresh cream, and Mary will have pears and custard.

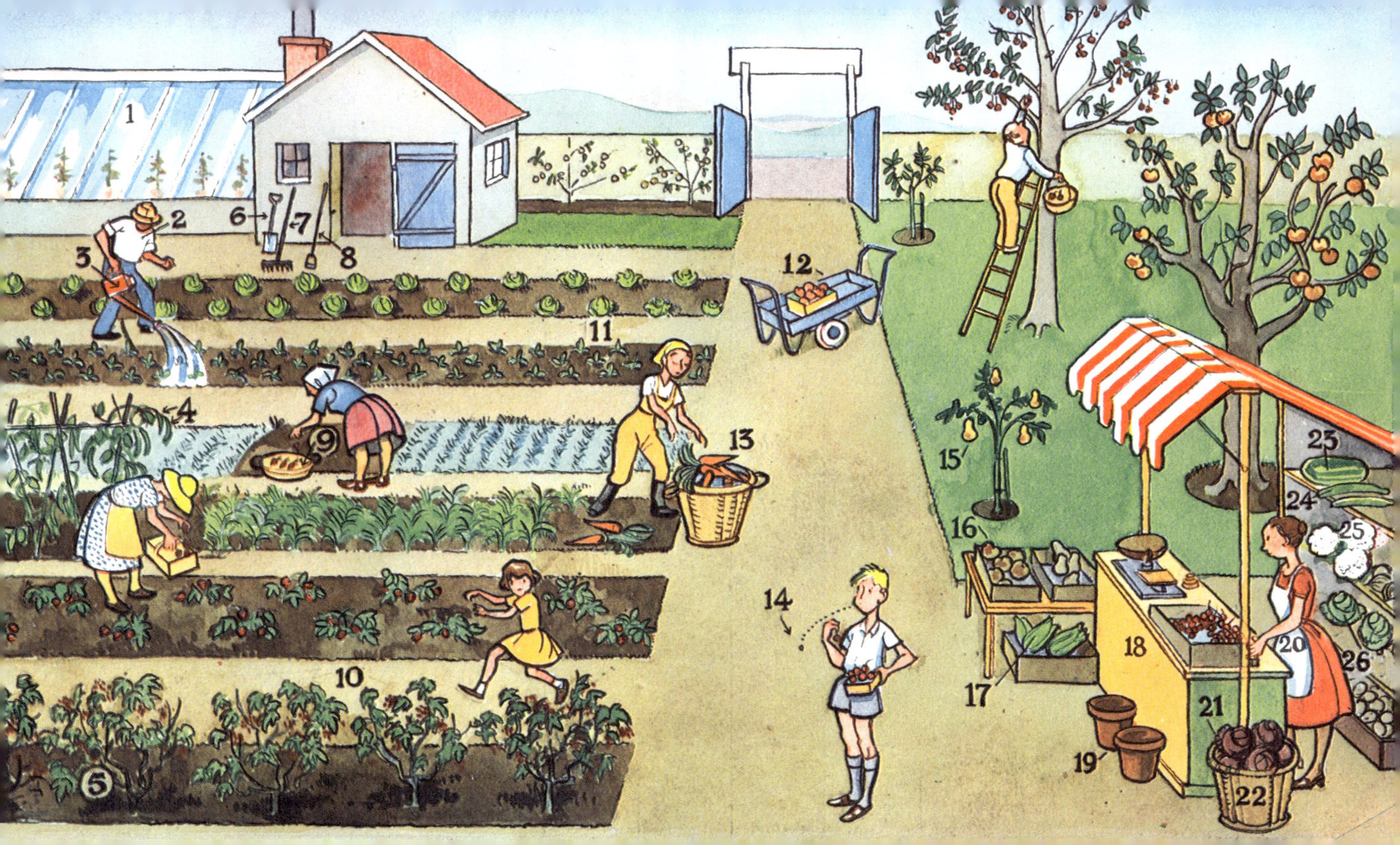
1
2
3
4
5
6
7
8
9
10
11
12
13
14
15
16
17
18
19
20
21
22
23
24
25
26

In the Tea-garden

1. Sun umbrella
2. Customer
3. Wallet
4. Money
5. Drinking-straw
6. Tumbler
7. Bill
8. Waitress
9. Lime tree
10. Table
11. Grandmother
12. Aunt
13. Scones
14. Tea-cup
15. Tea-pot
16. Fancy cakes
17. Grandfather
18. Car park
19. Hat
20. Tray
21. Plate
22. Meat
23. Spoon
24. Fork
25. Knife
26. Tea-room
27. Bay window
28. Camera
29. Tourist

Sometimes Mary and John are invited out to tea by their grandparents.

"If you are good," said their grandmother one day, "we'll take you to have tea in a lovely tea-garden."

The children were good. Their grandparents, therefore, took them to the tea-garden. Aunt Jean was invited too, so Mary and John were very happy.

The tea-room was in a large garden. There was a beautiful lime tree in the middle of it. They all sat at a table under the tree in the shade.

John and Mary tried not to look too hungry. Soon the scones, cakes, and all sorts of other nice things had arrived, and Grandmother was pouring out the tea.

"They certainly are lovely cakes," said Aunt Jean. "I shall get very fat if I eat too many of these."

"John's like me," said Grandfather. "He doesn't worry about his figure."

Both John and Mary thought the tea-garden was lovely. They hoped that their grandparents would take them there again.

CAR PARK
RIVERSIDE TEA ROO
1
2
3
4
5
6
7
8
9
10
11
12
13
14
15
16
17
18
19
20
21,22,23
24
25
26
27
28
29

On the Farm

1 Hen-house
2 Gangway
3 Farm-worker (land-girl)
4 Bucket
5 Hens
6 Mother hen
7 Chicks
8 Farmhouse
9 Kennel
10 Dog
11 Cock
12 Geese
13 Bill or beak
14 Farmyard
15 Cat
16 Ploughed land
17 Manure heap
18 Farmer
19 Pipe
20 Tractor
21 Barn
22 Loft
23 Trailer
24 Wheel
25 Pigeon
26 Ear of wheat
27 Pond
28 Duck

There is a farm about two miles away from the Browns' house. John knows the farmer who owns it. He spends most of his spare time in the farmyard. If the farmer is busy John helps him. Sometimes Mary goes with John to the farm. She loves the cats and dogs. She also likes going to the farmyard when there are some baby chicks.

"Why does the farmer have such a big garage?", asked Mary one day.

"Because he has so many tractors and so much machinery to look after," replied John.

There is a large dog in the yard. At first he did not like John. He used to growl when he saw him. Now he likes him and wags his tail when John strokes him.

The farmer grows crops, but he also keeps cows, hens, and geese. The geese hiss and flap their wings at everybody. The land-girl is afraid of them, but she likes the chickens.

"Can I help you collect the eggs?", asks Mary.

"Yes, of course, but be careful the hens don't peck you," replies the girl.

The farmer likes John because he is interested in farming.

"When you leave school," says the farmer, "you can come and help me on the farm."

John would like to do that, but his father wants him to pass all his examinations first.

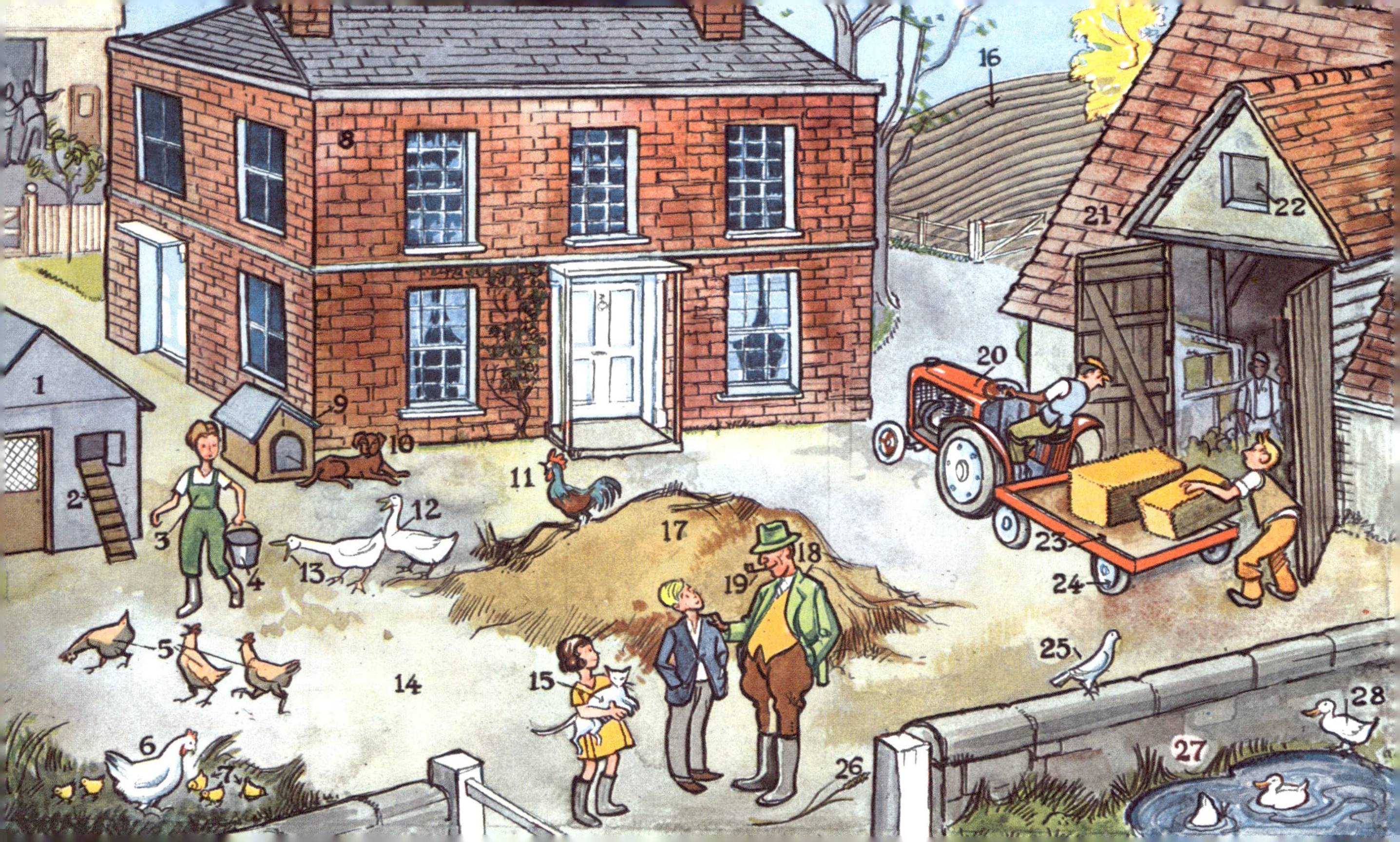
1
2
3
4
5
6
7
8
9
10
11
12
13
14
15
16
17
18
19
20
21
22
23
24
25
26
27
28

In the Cow-shed

1 Straw
2 Apron
3 Ladder
4 Bin
5 Cow
6 Udder
7 Milkmaid
8 Calf
9 Cord
10 Muzzle
11 Cowman
12 Fodder
13 Hay
14 Milk
15 Broom
16 Rubbish
17 Brush
18 Lamb
19 Sheep
20 Piglet
21 Trough
22 Pig

When the children visit the farm, Mary always goes to see the cows being milked. Sometimes the farmer lets her milk the cows herself. She likes doing this, though there is one cow called Sarah which she does not like. Sarah always hits Mary in the face with her tail and sometimes gets very angry and puts her hoof in her bucket.

There is another cow called Vera. She has a baby calf in the stall next to her own. She is always looking at the calf because she is very proud of her.

Both Mary and John like young animals better than old ones. They like the lambs better than the sheep, the piglets better than the big, fat pigs, and the calves better than the cows.

"Isn't it sweet!" Mary always says when she sees a baby animal.

John loves to feed the animals. One day he took a sandwich with him to a big shed in the farm. He offered it to a sheep, but the sheep turned its head away. Then he offered it to a pig. And the greedy pig ate it up straight away.

"Pigs will eat anything, they're so greedy," said John.

"Just like you!" said Mary. Then they began to fight and they both fell into the straw on the floor.

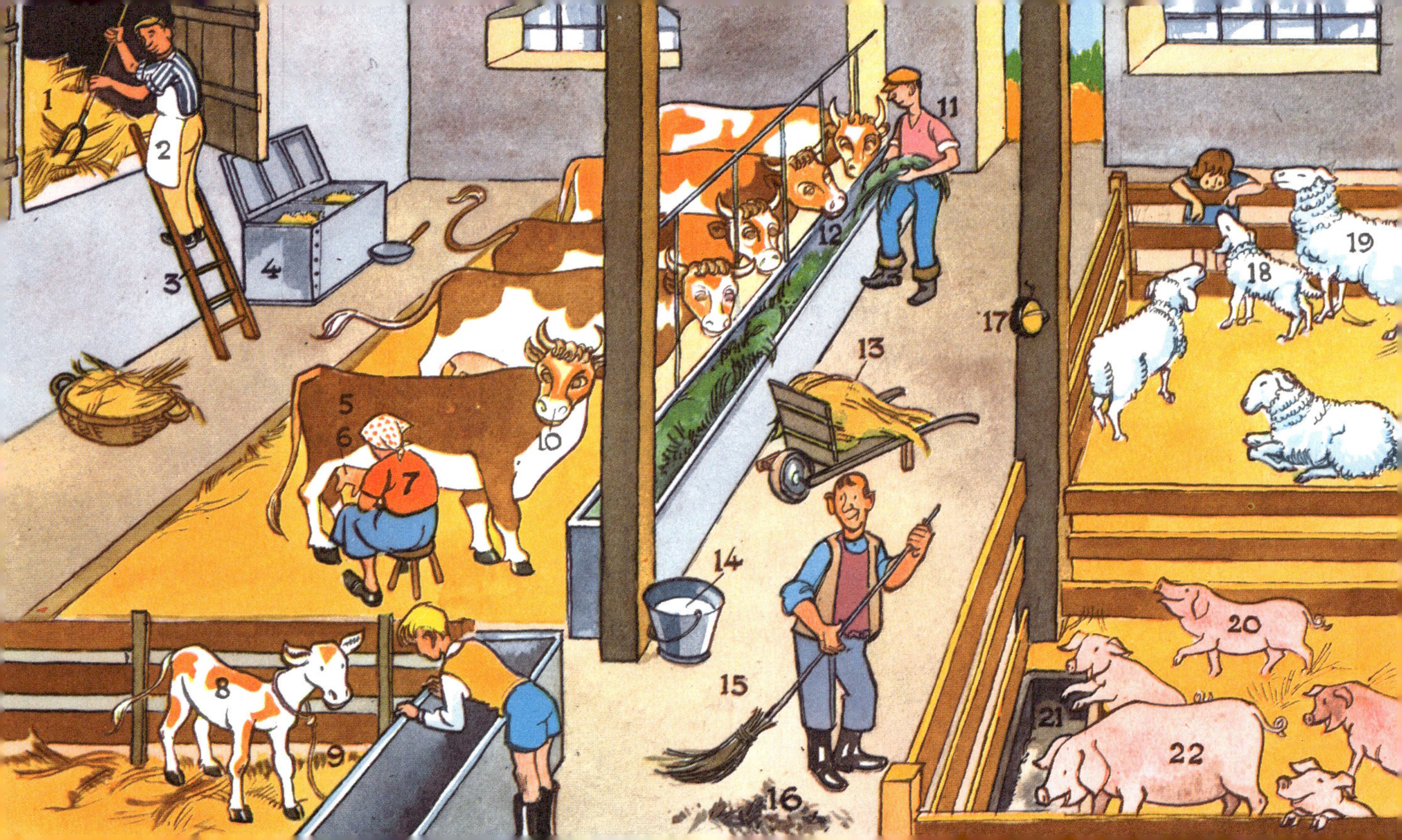
1
2
3
4
5
6
7
8
9
10
11
12
13
14
15
16
17
18
19
20
21
22

By the River

1 Poplar
2 Windmill
3 Hill
4 Bridge
5 Horseman
6 Hoof-marks
7 Horse
8 Reins
9 Path
10 Hare
11 Town
12 Field
13 Road
14 Motor-coach
15 Tent
16 Stool
17 Puddle
18 Lake
19 Dressing-rooms
20 Swimming-pool
21 Sail
22 Mast
23 Fishing rod
24 Landing-stage
25 Kettle
26 Paraffin stove
27 Sun
28 Embankment
29 Dust
30 Island
31 Jar
32 Net
33 Bank

Just outside the town where the Browns live there is a river. When it is too cold to swim in it they like to go fishing.

"What shall we do to-day?" asks John.

"Let's go fishing," says Mary.

It is a threepenny bus ride to the river. Mary and John can see the blue water below them from the top of the bus.

"Look," says Mary, "there are a lot of people here to-day."

The children walk down the path along the side of the river. On the way they see a man riding a horse—and a tent with all kinds of camping equipment.

"I wish we could camp by the river," says John.

"I shouldn't like it when it got dark," says Mary.

They both ran down to the river's edge and took off their shoes and socks.

"Don't make too much noise," says a fisherman nearby. "You'll frighten all the fish away."

"We'd better move farther along," says John, "or that gentleman might get angry."

1
2
3
4
5
6
7
8
9
10
11
12
13
14
15
16
17
18
19
20
21
22
23
24
25
26
27
28
29
30
31
32
33

At the Seaside

1 Smoke
2 Shadow
3 Aeroplane
4 Waves
5 Rowing-boat
6 Deck-chair
7 Sand
8 Bone
9 Lighthouse
10 Ship
11 Canoe
12 Sandcastle
13 Castle
14 Rock
15 Bay
16 Crane
17 Rope
18 Harbour

Mr Brown has a cottage by the sea. In August Mrs Brown takes the children to stay in the cottage for a week. The dog always goes too. He loves playing with the children on the beach and burying his bones in the garden.

When the weather is fine Mary and John spend the whole day on the beach. Mary helps John to make sandcastles. Mrs Brown, however, prefers to relax in a deck-chair. The cottage overlooks a small harbour. There is often a ship tied up at the quayside. The children like to watch the cargo being unloaded. There are always several yachts to be seen out at sea.

The children bathe every day. John is a strong swimmer, but Mrs Brown is always afraid that he will swim out too far.

"Be careful, John!" she shouts. "The sea is quite rough to-day, so don't swim out too far."

If it is too cold to bathe Mary and John go and explore the castle. It is about a mile away from the cottage.

Sometimes Mrs Brown allows John and Mary to hire a rowing-boat. But Mary soon gets tired and John gets cross with her.

"My arms ache," complains Mary, after she has been in the boat for about five minutes.

"You'd better climb out and go home," replies John. "After all, rowing is only for strong fellows like me."

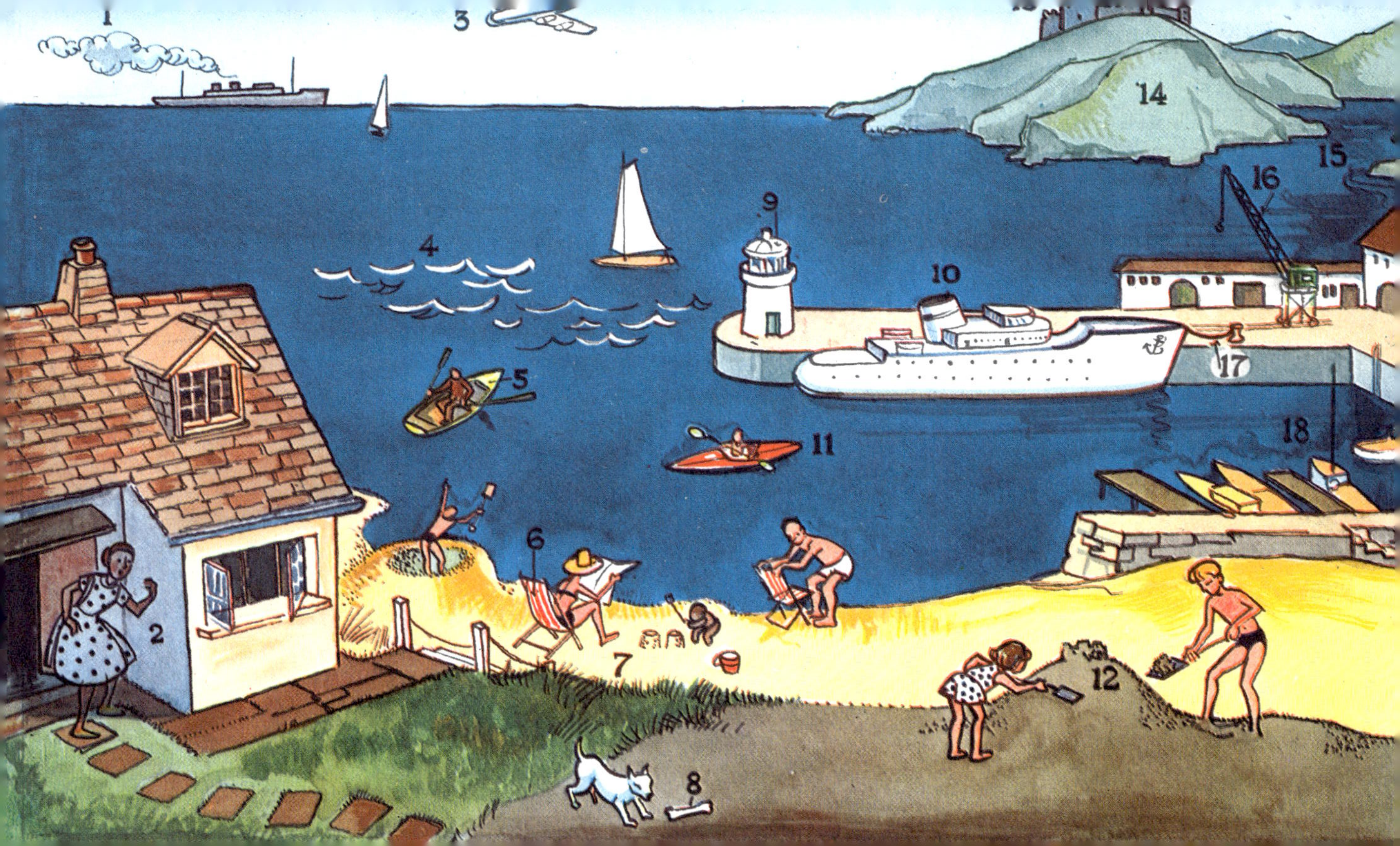
1
3
14
15
16
9
4
10
5
17
18
11
6
2
7
12
8

At the New House

1. Chimney
2. Bricklayer
3. Tiler
4. Window (opening)
5. Scaffolding
6. Cloud
7. Roof
8. Village
9. Tower
10. Garage
11. Shovel
12. Building site
13. Kite
14. Sheaf
15. Pasture
16. Shepherd
17. Crook
18. Sheep-dog
19. Flock
20. Bricks
21. Eagle
22. Mountain
23. Birch tree
24. Cap
25. Man
26. Stick

A new house is being built for the Browns in the country. Mary and John love to watch it being made. Each week there is another door or window added. Soon the roof will be finished.

"Won't it be lovely when we live here," says John. "We shall have all these fields to play in."

When they go to watch the house being built Mary and John often take their kite with them. They can fly it in the fields nearby. There are no other houses near the Browns' new house. They can see a village in the hills not far away. They will be able to see the church tower from their new garden.

One day there was an old shepherd in the field next to the house with a flock of sheep.

"Look, there is a shepherd!" cried Mary to John. "He has a lovely sheep-dog with him."

"Let's go and talk to him," said John.

John and Mary talked to the shepherd for a long time. He said that he would show them the countryside when they came to live in their new house.

The children wished that the builders would hurry and finish their new house. They wanted to live in it as quickly as possible.

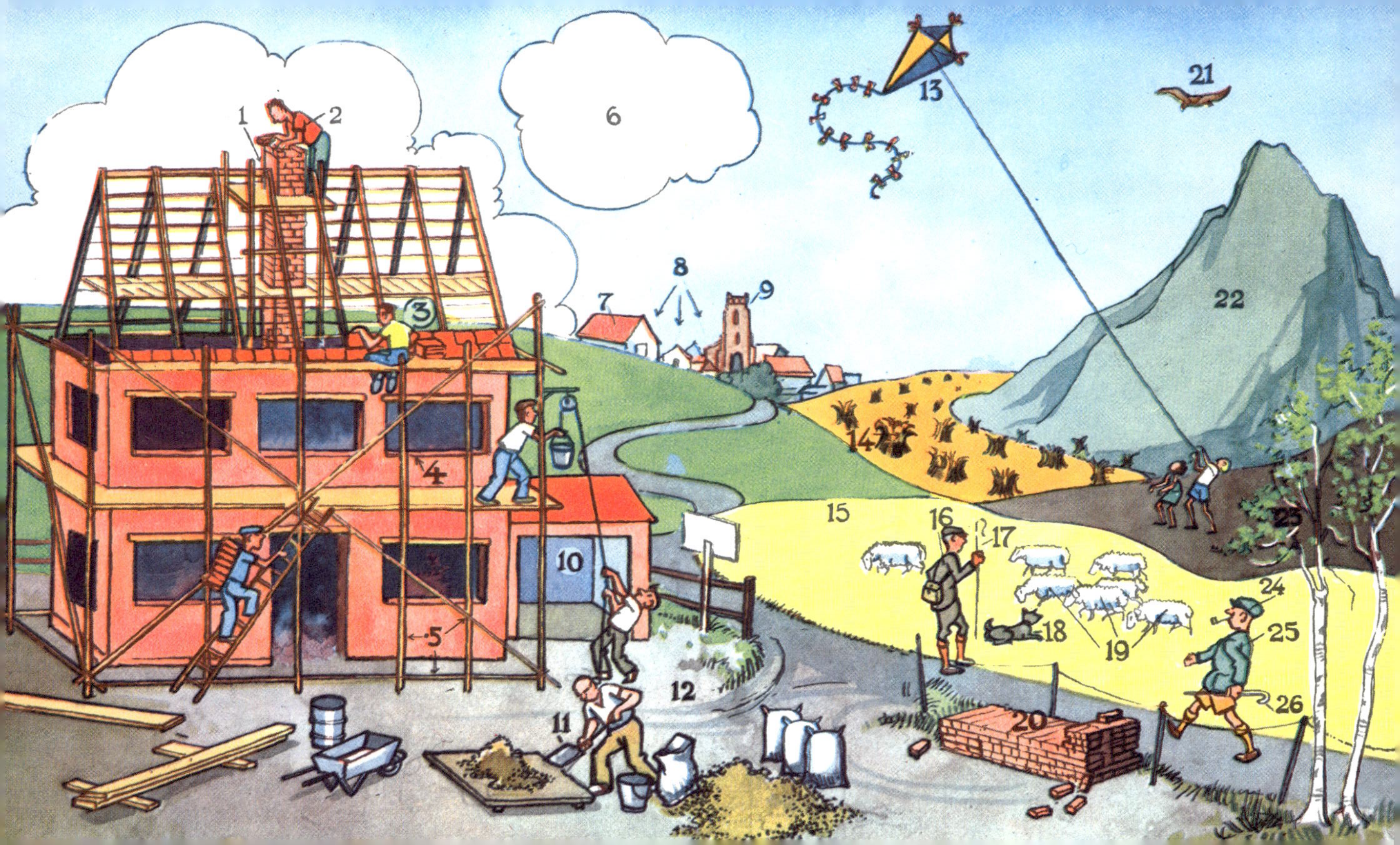
1
2
3
4
5
6
7
8
9
10
11
12
13
14
15
16
17
18
19
20
21
22
23
24
25
26

At the Station

1 Tunnel
2 Lightning
3 Railway carriage
4 Rail
5 Bag
6 Traveller
7 Booking office
8 Parcel
9 Buffers
10 Clock
11 Guard
12 Left luggage office
13 Suitcase
14 Compartment
15 Engine driver
16 Level crossing
17 Steam
18 Bus
19 Bus driver
20 Rain
21 Island
22 Boiler
23 Bus stop
24 Locomotive
25 Fence

Mary and John's grandmother often comes to stay. The family are very sad, however, when it is time for her to leave.

The last time she left the Browns' house there was a big thunderstorm.

"I wish you weren't going, Granny," said Mary.

"So do I, dear," replied her grandmother. "But I shall be coming again soon."

"Your train goes at 3.5 p.m., Granny, so we'd better hurry or you'll miss it," said John.

Granny said good-bye to Mr and Mrs Brown but the children went with her to the station. It was raining and the children got very wet.

While Granny was buying her ticket she asked Mary to hold her purse. At last she was ready to go.

The children said good-bye and ran out of the station. They saw a bus had stopped at the bus stop, so they jumped on it.

Suddenly Mary remembered that she had forgotten to give Granny back her purse. When the bus driver heard what had happened he stopped the bus and John and Mary ran back to the station.

They found their grandmother sitting on a seat waiting for her train. She was very pleased that they had brought back her purse.

BOOKING OFFICE
LEFT LUGGAGE OFFICE
BUS STOP

Great Britain and Ireland

1 Dublin
2 Belfast
3 Glasgow
4 Caernarvon
5 Plymouth
6 Swansea
7 Cardiff
8 Liverpool
9 Edinburgh
10 Bristol
11 Manchester
12 Aberdeen
13 Stoke-on-Trent
14 Wolverhampton
15 Birmingham
16 Stratford-on-Avon
17 Newcastle
18 Durham
19 Leeds
20 Sheffield
21 Leicester
22 Oxford
23 York
24 Portsmouth
25 Hull
26 Cambridge
27 London
28 Canterbury

One spring evening John and Mary asked their father where they were going for the summer holidays.

"I have not really decided yet," he said. "Let's look at a map of Great Britain."

John ran to the book shelf and took out his atlas. He turned the pages until he found the map.

"I should like to go to Scotland," suggested Mary.

"That is a good idea," said her father. "We can take the car with us, and then we can stop at some of the interesting towns on the way there."

"Shall we stay in Edinburgh?" asked Mrs Brown, who had always wanted to see the castle.

"Yes," said Mr Brown, "and perhaps we might go to Aberdeen for a few days."

"On the way to Scotland I should like to visit Stratford-on-Avon," said John. "We are doing one of Shakespeare's plays at school, and I would like to see where he was born."

"Stratford is a beautiful town," agreed Mr Brown. "Perhaps we might even see one of Shakespeare's plays in the famous theatre there."

John and Mary were very pleased with the holiday plans.

GREAT BRITAIN AND IRELAND

- 12 FISHING
- 17 COAL
- 20 CUTLERY / PLATE
- 22 CARS / UNIVERSITY
- 28 SEAT OF ARCHBISHOP / CATHEDRAL
- 9 SCOTTISH CAPITAL
- 19 CLOTHING
- 26 UNIVERSITY
- 27 HOUSES OF PARLIAMENT
- 2 LINEN
- 8 SHIPPING TRADE
- 13 POTTERY
- 16 SHAKESPEARE MEMORIAL THEATRE
- 3 SHIPBUILDING
- 11 COTTON GOODS
- 1 CAPITAL OF IRISH FREE STATE
- 14 ENGINEERING
- 7 CAPITAL OF WALES

The United States of America

1 San Francisco
2 Los Angeles
3 Seattle
4 Salt Lake City
5 Denver
6 Oklahoma City
7 Kansas City
8 Houston
9 Minneapolis
10 St Louis
11 New Orleans
12 Milwaukee
13 Chicago
14 Cincinnati
15 Detroit
16 Atlanta
17 Pittsburgh
18 Cleveland
19 Miami
20 Washington
21 Baltimore
22 Philadelphia
23 New York
24 Boston

Last term John's class at school began learning about the United States of America.

The teacher brought a large map with him and asked the boys to point out the towns they had heard about.

"I have an uncle who lives in Washington," said one of the boys.

"Washington is the capital city of America," said the master. "The President lives there in a large house called 'The White House.'"

The master asked many questions about America, and often John could answer them.

"Can you tell me anything about California, John?" asked his master.

John often goes to the cinema and he knows that films are made near Los Angeles, which is in California.

"The weather is always very hot there too," said John.

"Yes, that is true, but the most popular holiday resort is on the other side of America; it is called Miami," said his master.

"I should like to go to New York for a holiday," said one of John's friends. "I have heard so much about the skyscrapers there."

One of John's friends went to live in America and he sometimes writes to John.

UNITED STATES OF AMERICA

Vocabulary

This vocabulary teaches the student the meaning of words as used in this book. It contains all the words in the book except for those which appear in numbered lists opposite the illustrations.

Each word is used in a simple example so that its meaning will be obvious, and, where possible, examples are made up with words which are illustrated in the pictures.

The words are listed alphabetically, each followed by its phonetic transcription (in the International Phonetic Alphabet) and then by its part of speech

film (film) *n.*
 Let's go to the cinema and see the new film.

Only irregular plurals of *nouns* are indicated

fisherman (ˈfiʃəmən) *n.*—fishermen.
 The fisherman has a fishing-rod in his hands and tries to catch fish.

When no plural is indicated, the plural is made by adding -s. E.g., the plural of *cow* is *cows*.

Only irregular past tenses and past participles of *verbs* are given

begin (biˈgin) *vb.*—began, begun.

Past tenses and past participles are also cross-referenced in the vocabulary

came (keim) see **come**.

When no past tenses and past participles are given, they are formed by adding -ed to verb-roots ending with a **consonant**— e.g., end*ed*, end*ed*; or by adding -d to verb-roots ending with -e—e.g., love*d*, love*d*.

ABBREVIATIONS

plur. plural
conj. conjunction
adv. phr. adverbial phrase
superl. superlative
comp. comparative
n. phr. noun phrase
prep. phr. prepositional phrase
vb. phr. verbal phrase
int. interjection

aux. auxiliary
adj. adjective
adv. adverb
n. noun
pron. pronoun
prep. preposition
vb. verb
dem. pron. demonstrative pronoun
rel. pron. relative pronoun

poss. adj. possessive adjective

(to be) able (to) ('eibl tu(:)) *adj.* I cannot help you because I am not able to move my arm.

about (ə'baut) *adv.* I don't know how long it will take; about two weeks, I think.

about (ə'baut) *prep.* The teacher talked to us about France.

above (ə'bʌv) *adv.* The very last line is clearly written, but the line above is not.

ache (eik) *vb.* I was hit on the head and it still aches.

across (ə'krɔs) *prep.* I flew across the Atlantic to go from England to America.

act (ækt) *n.* The play is very short; it has only one act.

add (æd) *vb.* The potatoes were not salted enough, so Mother had to add some salt.

afford (ə'fɔːd) *vb.* He has just received some money, so now he can afford to buy a new car.

afraid (ə'freid) *adj.* Mary is afraid when the dog growls.

afraid (of) (ə'freid ɔv) *adj.* I don't want to go near that house because there is a dog and I am afraid of it.

after ('ɑːftə) *prep.* Summer comes after Spring.

afternoon (ˌɑːftə'nuːn) *n.* In the morning I went to church; then I had lunch, and in the afternoon I went to the park.

again (ə'gen) *adv.* Show it to me again so I can see it a second time.

against (ə'genst) *prep.* We played football against the other school.

ago (ə'gou) *adj.* I am now twelve years old; two years ago I was only ten.

agree (ə'griː) *vb.* We wanted to go to the zoo with Mother; she agreed and came with us.

all (ɔːl) *adj.* I was asked five questions and I knew all the answers.

allow (to) (ə'lau tu(:)) *vb.* Mother does not allow us to play by the river because it is too dangerous.

almost ('ɔːlmoust) *adv.* I arrived so late that I almost missed my train.

along (əˈlɔŋ) *prep.* Mary and John walked along the beach to follow the boat.

already (ɔːlˈredi) *adv.* Ten o'clock already! I didn't think it was so late.

also (ˈɔːlsou) *adv.* At the zoo you can see not only bears and monkeys but also tigers and lions.

always (ˈɔːlwəz) *adv.* I always take my umbrella when it rains.

angry (ˈæŋgri) *adj.* John was angry because he had to study so long that he missed the tennis match.

angry (with) (ˈæŋgri wið) *adj.* I am angry with Mary because she took my pen and lost it.

animal (ˈænimǝl) *n.* A cow is an animal.

annoy (əˈnɔi) *vb.* The dog barks when I pull its tail because it is annoyed.

another (əˈnʌðə) *adj.* May I have another cup of tea, please?

(one) another (wʌn əˈnʌðə) *pron.* John and Mary met again after they had been away from one another for two years.

answer (ˈɑːnsə) *n.* I asked him a question, but he didn't know the answer.

anything (ˈeniθiŋ) *pron. or n.* What was that noise? Has anything happened?

anyway (ˈeniwei) *adv.* I don't think I can reach it but I can try anyway.

apologize (əˈpɔlədʒaiz) *vb.* I was late for school, so I apologized to the teacher.

arrange (əˈreindʒ) *vb.* Mary bought some flowers, arranged them in a vase, and put them in the sitting-room.

arrive (əˈraiv) *vb.* I was expecting a parcel but it has not arrived yet.

ask (ɑːsk) *vb.* (1) I have to ask my mother if she will let me go with you. (2) John's mother asked me for dinner; may I go, please?

at (æt) *prep.* He is neither at home nor at school.

ate (et/eit) see **eat**.

atlas (ˈætləs) *n.*—atlases. In his atlas John can find maps of every country of the world.

at last (æt laːst) *adv. phr.* He tried and tried again, and at last he managed to do it.

August (ˈɔːgʌst) *n.* August is the eighth month of the year.

away (əˈwei) *adv.* John has gone to Africa; he has been away for two months now.

away (from) (əˈwei frɔm) *adv.* They live near us, only two streets away from here.

baby (ˈbeibi) *n.*—babies. Our little sister is two weeks old; she is only a baby.

back (bæk) *adv.* He forgot his pen, so he went back to school to get it.

(in the) **back** (of) (bæk ɔv) *prep. phr.* The farmer was putting vegetables in the back of his lorry.

badly (ˈbædli) *adv.* His homework was badly done and he had to do it again.

bakery (ˈbeikəri) *n.*—bakeries. A bakery is a shop where bread is sold.

bathe (beið) *vb.* If the water is not too cold we bathe in the sea.

beach (biːtʃ) *n.*—beaches. I like to lie on the beach after I have been swimming.

bear (bɛə) *vb.*—bore, borne. We have a new baby sister at home. She was born last week.

beat (biːt) *vb.*—beat, beaten. (1) Before you make an omelette you must beat the eggs well. (2) Peter beat John in the race and won the prize.

beaten (biːtn) see **beat**.

beautiful (ˈbjuːtiful) *adj.* They have a beautiful house. I would love to stay there.

because (biˈkɔz) *conj.* "Why are you late?" asked the teacher.
"Because I overslept," replied John.

bedroom (ˈbedrum) *n.* My bedroom is the room in which I sleep.

before (biˈfɔː) *prep.* I arrived before Mary because I ran.

began (biˈgæn) see **begin.**

begin (biˈgin) *vb.*—began, begun. The play will begin at seven o'clock, and finish at nine.

begun (biˈgʌn) see **begin.**

behind (biˈhaind) *prep.* John was hiding behind a tree.

belong to (biˈlɔŋ tu(ː)) *vb.* I found a toy in our garden and I gave it back to Mary because it belongs to her.

bench (bentʃ) *n.*—benches. Three old ladies were sitting on a bench in the park.

bend (down) (bend daun) *vb.*—bent, bent. I can bend down and touch my toes with my fingers.

bent (bent) see **bend.**

best (best) *adv.* She reads a lot about History because it is the subject she likes best.

best (best) *adj.*—*superl. of* good. He put on his best suit for the party.

better (ˈbetə) *adj.*—*comp. of* good. The first one is good, but the second is even better.

better (ˈbetə) *adv.* Don't try to teach me anything. I know it all better than you.

big (big) *adj.* I have a big brother who is five years older than me.

biology (baiˈɔlədʒi) *n.* In biology we learn all about animals.

birthday (ˈbəːθdei) *n.* To-day is my birthday. I am ten years old. Yesterday I was only nine.

blew (bluː) see **blow.**

blindfold (ˈblaindfould) *vb.* They put a handkerchief over John's eyes, and he could not see. He was blindfolded.

blow (out) (blou aut) *vb.*—blew, blown. Don't try to light a match in the wind. It will blow out.

blown (bloun) see **blow.**

blue (bluː) *adj.* The sky is blue.

board (bɔːd) *n.* Mary rolls out the pastry on a special board called a pastry-board.

born (bɔːn) see **bear**.

both (bouθ) *pron.* John and Peter were ill to-day, so both of them stayed at home.

bought (bɔːt) see **buy**.

boy (bɔi) *n.* Mary is a girl, John is a boy.

bread (bred) *n.* It's the baker who makes bread.

break (breik) *vb.*—broke, broken. I dropped my glass on the floor and it broke.

(to take a) **breath** (breθ) *vb. phr.* You take a big breath if you want to swim under water.

brief-case (ˈbriːfkeis) *n.* Father carries his papers in a brief-case.

bring (briŋ) *vb.*—brought, brought. I forgot to bring my pen so I have to use my pencil.

bring (back) (briŋ bæk) *vb.*—brought, brought. My shoes are still on the beach. I forgot to bring them back home.

bring (in) (briŋ in) *vb.*—brought, brought. We don't have enough chairs in this room. Could you bring another one in, please?

broke (brouk) see **break**.

brought (ˈbrɔːt) see **bring**.

build (bild) *vb.*—built, built. We often build sand castles on the beach.

builder (ˈbildə) *n.* A man who builds a house is a builder.

built (bilt) see **build**.

bunch (bʌntʃ) *n.*—bunches. I didn't get just one radish, but a whole bunch of them.

buried (ˈberid) see **bury**.

bury (ˈberi) *vb.*—buried, buried. The dog dug a hole in the sand to bury its bone.

busy (ˈbizi) *adj.* (1) I am busy helping Mother. I cannot come and play with you. (2) The shop was very busy to-day. There were too many people.

but (bʌt) *conj.* He said he was listening, but I know he was not.

buy (bai) *vb.*—bought, bought. With the money he received he bought two books.

by (bai) *prep.* It is not far. It is just by the school.

call (kɔːl) *vb.* (1) Mother called me for lunch, but I was too far away to hear her. (2) I am not sure of the dog's name, but I think he's called Pablo.

call (in) (kɔːl in) *vb.* On our way back home we called in at John's, but he wasn't there.

call (to) (kɔːl tu(ː)) *vb.* Mother called to Father that dinner was ready.

came (keim) see **come**.

camp (kæmp) *vb.* If we travel, we won't stay in hotels but we will take our tents and camp.

(to go) **camping** (ˈkæmpiŋ) *vb. phr.* When we go camping we sleep in a tent.

can (kæn) *vb. aux.*—could. Can I help you? Of course you can.

can't (kaːnt)=**cannot**.

capital (ˈkæpitl) *adj.* Paris is the capital city of France.

careful (ˈkɛəfʊl) *adj.* Be careful when you carry the eggs because they break easily.

carol (ˈkærəl) *n.* At Christmas time everybody sings carols.

carried (ˈkærɪə) see **carry**.

carry (ˈkæri) *vb.*—carried, carried. Father helped me to carry my chair into the other room because it was too heavy for me.

casualty department (ˈkæʒjuəlti dɪˈpɑːtmənt) *n. phr.* In the casualty department of a hospital, doctors look after people who have been hurt in accidents.

catch (kætʃ) *vb.*—caught, caught. He threw the ball to me. I didn't catch it, and it went into the water.

catch (hold of) (kætʃ hould ɔv) *vb.*—caught, caught. He thought he could run away, but we caught hold of him.

caught (kɔːt) see **catch**.

centre (ˈsentə) *n.* There is always a big stone in the centre of a peach.

certainly (ˈsəːtnli) *adv.* Ask Daddy. He certainly knows about it.

change (tʃeindʒ) *n.* I gave the grocer too much money, and he gave me some change back.

change (tʃeindʒ) *vb.* The traffic light is still red, but it will soon change and become green.

child (ˈtʃaild) *n.*—children. Mary and the other children are playing in the garden.

children (ˈtʃildren) see **child**.

choose (tʃuːz) *vb.*—chose, chosen. I don't know which one to take. It is very difficult to choose.

chose (tʃouz) see **choose**.

chosen (ˈtʃouzn) see **choose**.

Christmas (ˈkrisməs) *n.* Christmas is on December 25th.

church (tʃəːtʃ) *n.*—churches. We go to church on Sundays to say our prayers.

class (klɑːs) *n.*—classes. We are not a big class—only ten pupils.

clean (kliːn) *vb.* My shoes were dirty so I had to clean them.

clear (kliə) *adj.* The water is so clear to-day that we can see the fish in the river.

clever (ˈklevə) *adj.* Mary is a very clever girl. She is always top of her class.

climb (over) (klaim ˈouvə) *vb.* John climbed over the fence to see the rabbits.

close (ˈklous) *adv.* We were afraid of being lost, so we stayed close to each other.

closely (ˈklousli) *adv.* The stamp is very small; you have to look at it closely to read what is written on it.

clothes (klouðz) *n. plur.* After I had fallen into the river, all my clothes were wet.

cold (kould) *adj.* It's so cold outside that I must wear two pullovers.

collect (kəˡlekt) *vb.* (1) I have to collect all my toys before I go to bed. (2) Mary and John collect stamps.

coloured (ˡkʌləd) *adj.* Negroes are also called coloured people.

colourful (ˡkʌləful) *adj.* Your skirt is very colourful with its blues, yellows, greens, and reds.

come (kʌm) *vb.*—came, come. Come here and sit down !

come (in) (kʌm in) *vb.*—came, come. "Come in!" Mother said to the man standing by the door.

come (on) (kʌm ɔn) *vb.*—came, come. Come on! We have to go now.

come (over) (kʌm ˡouvə) *vb.*—came, come. John was on the other side of the street. When he saw me he came over to talk to me.

come (round) (kʌm raund) *vb.*—came, come. Uncle William is coming to see us to-morrow : he is going to come round to-morrow.

come (up) (kʌm ʌp) *vb.*—came, come. We were waiting at the corner of the street when we saw John coming up.

complain (kəˡmplein) *vb.* Peter complained to his mother that he felt ill.

concentrate (ˡkɔnsentreit) *vb.* If you stop looking around you will be able to concentrate on your work.

cook (kuk) *vb.* Mother is cooking the meat for dinner.

cornet (ˡkɔːnit) *n.* The ice-cream man put the ice-cream into a cornet for us to eat.

cottage (ˡkɔtidʒ) *n.* A cottage is a small English house in the country.

cotton (ˡkɔtn) *n.* We wear wool in the winter and cotton in the summer.

could (kud) see **can**.

counter (ˡkauntə) *n.* The grocer always stands behind his counter to serve us.

country ('kʌntri) *n.*—countries. (1) The United States and Great Britain are countries. (2) Towns are too hot during the summer; that's why we go to the country.

countryside ('kʌntri'said) *n.* On Sundays we like to drive to the countryside, away from the town.

couple ('kʌpl) *n.* He stayed at home for a couple of days: Monday and Tuesday.

cousin ('kʌzn) *n.* John and Mary are my cousins because their father is my mother's brother.

cream (kri:m) *n.* The cream is always at the top of a bottle of milk.

creep (kri:p) *vb.*—crept, crept. (1) We must creep in because if we make a noise we will wake the baby. (2) I watched a caterpillar creep across the path.

crept (krept) see **creep**.

cried (kraid) see **cry**.

crop (krɔp) *n.* We had a good crop of apples this year. We got so many that we had to sell them.

cross (krɔs) *adj.* She is cross with me because I broke her doll.

cross (krɔs) *vb.* You are not allowed to cross the road when the light is red.

cry (krai) *vb.*—cried, cried. (1) The baby cried so much last night that I couldn't sleep. (2) "Hello!" cried Mary when she saw us across the street.

cut (kʌt) *vb.*—cut, cut. Mother cuts the bread into slices.

cut (kʌt) *n.* The knife fell on his leg and made a deep cut.

dark (dɑ:k) *adj.* As it was dark in the room I turned the light on.

day (dei) *n.* Sunday is the first day of the week.

dear (diə) *adj.* I started the letter: "My dear Uncle."

decide (di'said) *vb.* Do you want to go swimming or not? Come on, decide.

decorate ('dekəreit) *vb.* Our classroom is decorated with paper-chains of different colours for the party.

deep (diːp) *adj.* The water is not deep in the pond. It does not even come up to my knees.

delicious (diˈliʃəs) *adj.* These apples look so delicious that I can't wait to eat one.

delight (diˈlait) *vb.* I love chocolates and I was delighted because my aunt gave me some to-day.

department (diˈpɑːtmənt) *n.* I couldn't see any socks in the shop, and the assistant told me I was in the wrong department.

did (did) see **do.**

didn't (didnt) = **did not.**

different (ˈdifrənt) *adj.* We can find our sweaters easily because they are so different in colour.

difficult (ˈdifikəlt) *adj.* This book is too difficult for me. I don't understand it.

dining-room (ˈdainiŋrum) *n.* When we have guests we always eat in the dining-room and not in the kitchen.

dirt (dəːt) *n.* Mary decided to clean her bicycle because it was covered with dirt.

dish (diʃ) *n.*—dishes. After dinner, John and Mary help their mother to wash the dishes.

distance (ˈdistəns) *n.* I walked a long distance to-day: five miles.

do (duː) *vb.*—did, done. Mary helped her mother. She did the washing-up and made her bed.

doesn't (ˈdʌznt) = **does not.**

done (dʌn) see **do.**

don't (dount) = **do not,** see **do.**

downstairs (ˈdaunˈstɛəz) *adv.* Mary lives on the second floor. She has to go downstairs to answer the telephone, which is on the first floor.

dress (up) (dres ʌp) *vb.* Mr Brown dressed up as Father Christmas. He wore a red suit and a red cap, and had a long white beard.

dressing (ˈdresiŋ) *n.* The nurse puts a dressing on the cut to keep out the dirt.

drink (driŋk) *n.* A glass of lemonade is a refreshing drink.

drive (draiv) *vb.*—drove, driven. Peter's older brother can drive a car and he likes to go very fast.

driven ('drivn) see **drive**.

drop (drɔp) *vb.*—dropped, dropped. I dropped a glass on the floor and it broke.

dropped (drɔpt) see **drop**.

drove (drouv) see **drive**.

during ('djuəriŋ) *prep.* I won't see Peter during the winter as he will be away.

each (iːtʃ) *adj.* He was carrying two glasses, one in each hand.

early ('əːli) *adv.* Small children have to go to bed early.

eat (iːt) *vb.*—ate, eaten. At the party I drank a glass of lemonade and ate a piece of cake.

eaten ('iːtn) see **eat**.

edge (edʒ) *n.* Don't leave your glass on the edge of the table. It will fall on to the floor.

end (end) *n.* I am almost at the end of my book. I have only five more pages to read.

enter ('entə) *vb.* As the door was open, I entered the room.

equipment (i'kwipmənt) *n.* If you want to go camping, you want some camping equipment: a tent, a small stove, etc.

especially (is'peʃəli) *adv.* Peter likes cakes, especially chocolate cakes.

even ('iːvən) *adv.* Even on hot days the water is too cold to go swimming.

evening ('iːvniŋ) *n.* In the evening, after supper, Daddy always reads his newspaper.

every ('evri) *adj.* We go to school every day except on Saturdays and Sundays.

everybody ('evribɔdi) *pron.* It started raining and everybody ran into the house.

every one (ˈevriwʌn) *pron.* Of course I know him. Every one knows him.

everything (ˈevriθiŋ) *pron.* We didn't have everything with us since we had forgotten the cake for the picnic.

exam (igˈzæm) = **examination.**

examination (igˌzæmiˈneiʃən) *n.* The examination at the end of the year will show whether you have worked hard or not.

examine (igˈzæmin) *vb.* Father examined my bicycle carefully to see what was wrong with it.

excited (ikˈsaitid) *adj.* Mary was so excited when she went on holiday that she almost forgot to take some money with her.

excitedly (ikˈsaitidli) *adv.* After the accident Peter talked so excitedly that we couldn't understand a word of what he was saying.

exciting (ikˈsaitiŋ) *adj.* The film was so exciting I couldn't sleep afterwards.

exclaim (iksˈkleim) *vb.* "Oh! how marvellous!" exclaimed Mary after the party.

excuse (iksˈkjuːs) *n.* Tom doesn't like to work. He always has excuses.

explore (iksˈplɔː) *vb.* There was a part of the wood they had never seen, so they went to explore it.

fall (fɔːl) *vb.*—fell, fallen. The vase fell on the floor and broke.

fallen (ˈfɔːlən) see **fall.**

family (ˈfæmili) *n.*—families. There are four people in John's family: John and Mary and their father and mother.

famous (ˈfeiməs) *adj.* He is so famous that he is known all over the world.

far (fɑː) *adv.* It's too far to walk. We'll have to go by car.

far (away) (fɑː əˈwei) *adv. phr.* Peter lives far away, and it takes a long time to get to his house.

fascinate (ˈfæsineit) *vb.* I was so fascinated by the film that I didn't see anybody around me.

fast (fɑːst) *adj.* The fast train takes thirty minutes less than the slow train.

fastest (ˈfɑːstist) *adj., superl. of* **fast.**

fat (fæt) *adj.* Our dog eats too much and he is getting very fat.

favourite (ˈfeivərit) *n.* I like all kinds of jam, but strawberry jam is my favourite. I could eat some every day.

fed (fed) see **feed.**

feed (fiːd) *vb.*—fed, fed. We feed the dog three times a day, but he is always hungry.

feel (fiːl) *vb.*—felt, felt. (1) I could feel the heat from the fire. (2) I don't feel well to-day. I think I must go and see the doctor.

fell (fel) see **fall.**

fellow (ˈfelou) *n.* John met another fellow from his class and they played tennis together.

felt (felt) see **feel.**

few (fjuː) *adj.* I'll be ready in a few minutes.

fierce (fiəs) *adj.* The lion looks fierce when he roars.

fight (fait) *vb.*—fought, fought. Our dog likes to fight with other dogs. He often wins.

figure (ˈfigə) *n.* Mary has a nice figure. She is tall and slim.

film (film) *n.* Let's go to the cinema and see the new film.

finally (ˈfainli) *adv.* We waited twenty minutes for John, who finally arrived saying that the bus was late.

find (faind) *vb.*—found, found. I lost my pen and looked for it, but couldn't find it anywhere.

fine (fain) *adj.* (1) Yesterday John was not well, but to-day he feels fine. (2) The weather is fine when the sun shines.

finish (ˈfiniʃ) *vb.* When Mary had finished her homework, she went to see her friend Peggy.

fire (ˈfaiə) *n.* When it's cold we make a nice fire in the fireplace.

first (fəːst) *adj.* I have never been to a circus before. To-day will be the first time.

first (fəːst) *adv.* You have two things to do: first wash your hands and then clean your teeth.

fish (fiʃ) *vb.* I don't like to go fishing. I never catch any fish.

fisherman (ˈfiʃəmən) *n.*—fishermen. The fisherman has a fishing rod in his hands and tries to catch fish.

fit (fit) *vb.*—fitted, fitted. Mother is making a dress for me. I hope it will fit.

fit (fit) *adj.*—Mary is ill; she is not fit enough to come camping with us.

fitted (fitid) see **fit.**

flap (flæp) *vb.*—flapped, flapped. He was flapping his arms as if they were a bird's wings.

flapped (flæpt) see **flap.**

flew (fluː) see **fly.**

flour (ˈflauə) *n.* Bread is made with flour.

flower-bed (ˈflauəbed) *n.* The piece of garden where we grow flowers is called a flower-bed.

flown (floun) see **fly.**

fly (flai) *vb.*—flew, flown. The plane flew so high that we could hardly see it.

fly (something) (flai) *vb.*—flew, flown. I flew my kite so high that I could hardly see it.

fold (fould) *vb.* The letter did not fit in the envelope, so I folded it.

fond (of) (fɔnd ɔv) *adj.* Mary is so fond of her dolls. She doesn't play with anything else.

food (fuːd) *n.* We have plenty of food to eat.

for (fɔː) *prep.* A letter arrived and it is for me.

forget (fəˈget) *vb.*—forgot, forgotten. I forgot to bring my pencil this morning, so I had nothing to write with at school.

forgot (fəˈgɔt) see **forget**.

forgotten (fəˈgɔtn) see **forget**.

fought (fɔːt) see **fight**.

found (faund) see **find**.

fresh (freʃ) *adj.* (1) These vegetables are very fresh. We have just picked them from the garden. (2) These towels have just been washed. They have a fresh, clean smell.

friend (frend) *n.* The children I play with and I invite to my party are my friends.

frighten (ˈfraitn) *vb.* John hid under my bed to try to frighten me.

frighten (away) (ˈfraitn əˈwei) *vb.* The dog barked at the birds and frightened them away.

frightened (of) (ˈfraitnd ɔv) *adj.* I don't like dogs. I am frightened of them.

from (frɔm) *prep.* I received this book from my grandmother.

(in) **front** (of) (in frʌnt ɔv) *prep. phr.* I could see him very well. He was right in front of me.

fruit (fruːt) *n.* I feel like eating some fruit. I'll have an apple.

full (ful) *adj.* My basket was so full that I couldn't put another parcel in it.

further (ˈfəːðə) *adv.* We have not gone far yet; let's go further.

further (along) (ˈfəːðə əˈlɔŋ) *adv.* Mary lives in the same street, but a little further along.

game (geim) *n.* When it rains we stay at home and play all sorts of games.

gardening (ˈgɑːdniŋ) *n.* My parents like gardening on Saturday afternoons because they can do a lot of work in the garden then.

gave (geiv) see **give**.

gentle (ˈdʒentl) *adj.* Our dog is as gentle as a lamb.

gentleman (ˈdʒentlmən) *n.*—gentlemen. Our new neighbours are a French gentleman and his wife.

gently (ˈdʒentli) *adv.* The doctor examined my elbow very gently. He didn't want to hurt me.

geography (dʒiˈɔgrəfi) *n.* When you study Geography you learn about other countries.

get (get) *vb*—got, got. I'll be ten to-morrow. I am getting older.

get (in) (get in) *vb.*—got, got. The bus was very full; I only just got in.

get (into) (get ˈintu(ː)) *vb.*—got, got. We managed to get into the station before it started raining.

get (off) (get ɔ(ː)f) *vb.*—got, got. The bus will stop at the next street. We'll get off there.

get (up) (get ʌp) *vb.*—got, got. When I am on holiday, I like to stay in bed late; I never get up before ten o'clock

girl (gəːl) *n.* This little girl is my sister.

give (giv) *vb.*—gave, given. Please give me another piece of bread. I am still hungry.

give (back) (giv bæk) *vb.*—gave, given. You can use my pen but give it back to me as soon as you have finished with it.

given (ˈgivn) see **give**.

go (gou) *vb.*—went, gone. On Saturdays I always go to the park to play.

go (back) (gou bæk) *vb.*—went, gone. Mary is afraid when it is dark. She does not like to go back home all alone.

go (off) (gou ɔ(ː)f) *vb.*—went, gone. He went off to Africa yesterday.

go (out) (gou aut) *vb.*—went, gone. He went out of the room and did not come back.

gone (gɔːn) see **go**.

good (gud) *adj.* Come on now! Be a good boy.

good-bye (gud'bai) *n. int.* Daddy leaves early in the morning, so I get up to say good-bye to him.

good morning (gud 'mɔːniŋ) *n. phr.* Every morning when we arrive in the classroom we say "Good morning" to the master.

good night ('gud 'nait) *n. phr.* The little boy said good night when he went to bed.

got (gɔt) see **get**.

grandparent ('græn,pɛərənt) *n.* My grandmother and my grandfather are my grandparents.

granny ('græni) *n.*—grannies. Children usually call their grandmother "Granny."

great (greit) *adj.* Peter and John are great friends.

greedy (griːdi) *adj.* That boy is very greedy. If he eats much more he will be ill.

green (griːn) *adj.* The leaves on the trees are green during the summer.

greengrocer ('griːn,grousə) *n.* In the market we buy our vegetables at the greengrocer's stall.

grew (gruː) see **grow**.

groceries ('grousəriz) *n. pl.* The grocer sells all sorts of groceries—salt, sugar, rice, cheese, etc.

grow (grou) *vb.*—grew, grown. We grow tulips in our garden.

growl (graul) *vb.* The dog will growl if anyone comes near him when he is eating a bone.

grown (groun) see **grow**.

gruffly (grʌfli) *adv.* When our teacher is angry he talks gruffly.

guest (gest) *n.* My aunt came with us during the summer; she was our guest for a whole week.

hand (hænd) *vb.* Please hand me your reader, John.

happen ('hæpən) *vb.* What happens at the end of the film?

happy ('hæpi) *adj.* I am so happy. I have won the prize.

hasn't (hæznt) = **has not.**

have (hæv, həv) *vb.*—had, had. I have two brothers and two sisters.

have (to) (hæftə, hæftu) *vb.*—had, had. We have to go now if we want to be in time.

heal (hi:l) *vb.* Peter hurt his leg and it took three weeks to heal.

hear (hiə) *vb.*—heard, heard. Speak up! I can't hear a word.

hear (about) (hiə ə'baut) *vb.*—heard, heard. I heard about your leaving the town. Is it true?

heard (hə:d) see **hear.**

held (held) see **hold.**

help (help) *vb.* I cannot carry this suitcase by myself. Could you help me please?

her (hə:) *adj.* Mary invited her friends to a party.

here (hiə) *adv.* Peter is not here. He has just gone to the park.

hers (hə:z) *pron.* Mary kept the book because she said it was hers.

herself (hə:'self) *pron.* Her father didn't help her. She made it all by herself.

hide (haid) *vb.*—hid, hidden. When I play with the dog I hide a bone and he looks everywhere to find it.

high (hai) *adj.* The ceiling is so high that I cannot touch it.

himself (him'self) *pron.* When John saw himself in the mirror he noticed that his face was dirty.

hinge (hin*dʒ*) *n.* A door turns on hinges.

hire ('haiə) *vb.* You can hire a rowing-boat for twenty-five pence an hour.

his (hiz) *adj.* John forgot his book. He had to borrow Peter's.

his (hiz) *pron.* Mary couldn't find her pen and she asked Peter if she could use his.

hiss (his) *vb.* A goose hisses when it is annoyed.

history (ˈhistəri) *n.* In our history lesson to-day we read about Napoleon.

hit (hit) *vb.*—hit, hit. He hit my leg with his hockey stick and now it hurts.

hoe (hou) *vb.*—hoed, hoed. To have nice lettuce we have to hoe the garden to kill the weeds.

hold (hould) *vb.*—held, held. Charles held my school-bag while I tried to climb over the fence.

hold (up) (hould ʌp) *vb.*—held, held. The traffic didn't move. It was held up at a red light.

hole (houl) *n.* The fox lives in a hole.

holiday (ˈholədi/ˈholədei) *n.* For our Summer holidays we go to the sea.

home (houm) *adv.* Mary felt ill, so she went home to bed.

home-grown (ˈhoumˈgroun) *adj.* Our potatoes are home-grown. We don't buy them, we grow them in our garden.

home-made (ˈhoumˈmeid) *adj.* Home-made jam is the jam your mother makes at home.

hoof (hu:f) *n.*—hooves. Cows don't have feet. They have hooves.

hope (houp) *vb.* I hope that John will come back to-day, because I must see him before to-morrow.

horizon (həˈraizn) *n.* The horizon is the line where the earth and the sky seem to meet.

hot (hot) *adj.* The sun is always so hot.

how (hau) *adv.* I had to answer these questions: How are you? How do you like your school? How old are you? etc.

however (hauˈevə) *conj.* I like eating apples. Too many are not good for me, however.

hungry (ˈhʌŋgri) *adj.* I am not hungry at all. I don't want to eat anything.

hurried (ˈhʌrid) see **hurry.**

hurry (ˈhʌri) *vb.*—hurried, hurried. She hurried to finish her work to be able to go away earlier.

hurt (hə:t) *vb.*—hurt, hurt. Charles hurt his leg when he fell off his bicycle, but luckily it was not broken.

hutch (hʌtʃ) *n.*—hutches. We keep our rabbits in a hutch.

idea (aiˈdiə) *n.* Peter didn't tell me where he was going, and I have no idea where he could be.

I'm (aim) = **I am.**

important (imˈpɔːtənt) *adj.* This piece of paper is not important. You may throw it away.

in (in) *prep.* Your coat is in the cupboard.

indeed (inˈdiːd) *adv.* Do you like ice cream? I do indeed!

ink-blot (ˈiŋk-blɔt) *n.* My pen leaked and made ink-blots all over my work.

interested (ˈntristid) *adj.* My brother is interested only in detective stories. He does not read other stories.

interesting (ˈintristiŋ) *adj.* I did not like this book; it was not at all interesting.

interrrupt (ˌintəˈrʌpt) *vb.* Don't interrupt me while I am talking.

into (ˈintu) *prep.* Before you walk into the house you have to wipe your feet.

invite (inˈvait) *vb.* Mother invited Grandmother for dinner to-night.

item (ˈaitem) *n.* Mother had only four items on her shopping-list: salt, eggs, butter, and rice.

juicy (ˈdʒuːsi) *adj.* The oranges are not very juicy. They are almost dry inside.

July (dʒuːˈlai) *n.* July is the seventh month of the year.

jump (dʒʌmp) *n.* (1) The cat had to take a very big jump from the roof into the garden. (2) The horse missed the jump and fell.

jump (dʒʌmp) *vb*. This fence is so low that I can jump over it.

just (dʒʌst) *adv*. (1) I cannot do it just now. I'll do it later. (2) You asked for some new tennis balls. I have just what you want. (3) John got up so late that he just managed to catch his train.

keen (ki:n) *adj*. I shall go another day. I am not really keen to go to-day.

keen (on) (ki:n ɔn) *adj*. John is so keen on cricket that he goes to every match they play in his village.

keep (ki:p) *vb*.—kept, kept. Mother doesn't want us to keep a dog at home because she wouldn't have time to look after one.

kept (kept) see **keep**.

kind (kaind) *n*. At the market you can see all kinds of vegetables.

kind (kaind) *adj*. His mother is so kind, she prepared everything for us.

kitchen (ˈkitʃin) *n*. The kitchen is where one does the cooking.

knew (nju:) see **know**.

know (nou) *vb*.—knew, known. Mary did not know where.

know (about) (nou əˈbaut) *vb*.—knew, known. You don't have to tell me any more. I know everything about it.

known (noun) see **know**.

lady (ˈleidi) *n*.—ladies. Do you know that lady? She is John's mother.

laid (leid) see **lay**.

large (lɑ:dʒ) *adj*. This chair is large enough for me and Mary to sit on side by side.

last (lɑːst) *adj.* It's the first week of our holidays. Last week we were still at school.

late (leit) *adv.* He arrived late at the cinema and missed half of the film.

late (leit) *adj.* It was late last night when I went to bed. It was eleven o'clock.

lawn (lɔːn) *n.* The lawn is the piece of ground, covered with grass, around the house.

lay (lei) *vb.*—laid, laid. Mary is old enough to lay the table. She puts out all the forks, spoons, knives, and glasses before meals.

learn (ləːn) *vb.*—learned, learned. When we first go to school we learn our alphabet.

learnt (ləːnt) = **learned,** see **learn.**

leave (liːv) *vb.*—left, left. (1) The train arrived early but will leave late. (2) He ate the whole cake and didn't leave any for me.

leave (over) (liːv ˈouvə) *vb.*—left, left. We ate everything; nothing was left over from the meal.

left (left) see **leave.**

lesson (ˈlesn) *n.* I stayed at home Monday morning and missed the music lesson.

let (let) *vb.*—let, let. Let me try your new bicycle.

let's (lets) = **let us.**

lift (lift) *vb.* Daddy took the baby in his hands and lifted him up in the air.

light (lait) *vb.*—lit, lit. When you smoke you need a match to light your cigarette.

like (laik) *vb.* I like swimming so much that I go to the pool every day, even when it rains.

like (laik) *adj.* My brother is like me. We both are tall with brown hair and blue eyes.

list (list) *n.* The teacher keeps a list of all our names.

lit (lit) see **light.**

(a) **little** ('litl) *adv.* Don't go now! Stay a little longer.

live (liv) *vb.* Where do you live? I live in London.

local ('loukəl) *adj.* The local shops are the shops near us or in our village.

long to (lɔŋ tu) *vb.* I haven't seen Mother for a month. I am longing to see her.

long (lɔŋ) *adj.* It took me a long time to do my work and it is not even well done.

(no) **longer** ('lɔŋgə) *adv.* When John saw that it was raining he no longer wanted to go to the beach.

longingly ('lɔŋiŋli) *adv.* John wanted the cherries very much. He looked at them longingly.

look (luk) *vb.* Look, John, I have a new bicycle!

look (luk) *vb.* Peter looks very tired. I think it is time to send him to bed.

look (after) (luk ˑftə) *vb.* Mary likes cats very much, so she looks after our cat when we are on holiday.

look (at) (luk æt) *vb.* I am not touching the flowers. I am just looking at them.

look (forward to) (luk 'fɔːwəd tu) *vb.* I haven't seen my sister for two years. She arrives to-night. I'm looking forward to seeing her.

lose (luːz) *vb.*—lost, lost. I can't find my gloves anywhere. I think I've lost them.

lost (lɔst) see **lose**.

lot (of) (lɔt ɔv) *n.* I can't go out to play. I have a lot of things to do.

lots (lɔts) *n. in pl. (slang).* Yesterday I had nothing to do, but to-day I have lots to do.

loud (laud) *adj.* The music was so loud that we could hear it from across the street.

loudly ('laudli) *adv.* The teacher does not speak loudly enough. We can't hear him at the back of the classroom.

love (lʌv) *vb.* I love dogs. I would like to have one of my own.

lovely (ˈlʌvli) *adj.* I saw a lovely blue dress in the shop and I think you would like it.

luck (lʌk) *n.* I have had no luck to-day. I have lost all my money.

lucky (ˈlʌki) *adj.* Peter is lucky. He is allowed to go to the fair, but Mary and I are not.

lunch (lʌntʃ) *n.*—lunches. We usually have lunch at one o'clock.

machinery (məˈʃiːnəri) *n.* Modern farms have tractors, trailers, and many other pieces of machinery.

Mackintosh (ˈmækintɔʃ) *n.* A raincoat is called a Mackintosh or a mac.

made (meid) see **make**.

main (mein) *adj.* We didn't go to the sea for two reasons: the main one was that my father was ill; the other was that the weather was bad.

make (meik) *vb.*—made, made. (1) To help my mother I make my bed in the morning. (2) John never washes his hands. His mother has to make him do it.

manage (ˈmænidʒ) *vb.* I can easily manage to carry those two parcels; they are not heavy.

many (ˈmeni) *adj.* There were so many people in the room that we couldn't move.

marvellous (ˈmɑːviləs) *adj.* We had a marvellous holiday. The weather was just perfect.

match (mætʃ) *n.*—matches. There is a hockey match tomorrow. Daddy and I are going to watch it.

may (mei) *vb. aux.*—might. Peter asked his mother: "May I go and play with John now?"

mean (miːn) *vb.*—meant, meant. John hurt his sister by accident. He really didn't mean to.

meantime (ˈmiːnˈtaim) *n.* I must wait for John. In the meantime I'll eat a banana.

measure (ˈmeʒə) *vb.* I don't know how long this room is. I will have to measure it.

meet (miːt) *vb.*—met, met. I am going to the station to meet John, and we will both take the train.

mend (mend) *vb.* There is a hole in my sock. I'll have to ask Mother to mend it.

merry (ˈmeri) *adj.* On 25th December I wish everybody I see a very merry Christmas.

met (met) see **meet.**

mid-air (ˈmid ˈɛə) *n.* Peter threw the ball, and John jumped to catch it in mid-air.

middle (ˈmidl) *n.* The policeman stands in the middle of the street to direct the traffic.

might (mait) see **may.**

milk (milk) *vb.* We milk our cows with machines.

minute (ˈminit) *n.* There are sixty minutes in an hour.

miss (mis) *vb.* John arrived too late at the station and missed his train.

moment (ˈmoumənt) *n.* Wait for me, I will be back in a moment.

month (mʌnθ) *n.* January is the first month of the year.

more (mɔː) *adj.* I need more socks. I have only one pair left.

more (mɔː) *adv.* If I run more quickly I shall catch the bus.

morning (ˈmɔːniŋ) *n.* I got up early this morning.

most (moust) *adj.* or *n.* I don't like all the stories in this book, but I like most of them.

move (muːv) *vb.* The table was so heavy we could not even move it.

mow (mou) *vb.*—mowed, mown. The grass was long, so I helped Daddy to mow it.

mown (moun) see **mow.**

much (mʌtʃ) *adv.* How is John to-day? He is much better.

much (mʌtʃ) *adj.* He gave me too much milk and I couldn't drink it all.

(how) **much** (hau mʌtʃ) *adj.* or *n.* I don't know how much money I have in my wallet.

much (mʌtʃ) *n.* There is so much to see at the zoo that we didn't have time to see everything.

must (mʌst) *vb. aux.* You must be ready at four o'clock, otherwise you won't come with us.

nasty (ˈnɑːsti) *adj.* I don't like that drink: it has a nasty taste.

near (niə) *prep.* The rabbit came so near the fence that we could almost touch it.

nearby (niəˈbai) *adv.* My friend Peter doesn't live far from here. He lives nearby.

nearly (ˈniəli) *adv.* Nearly all my friends are ill to-day. Only John is well.

need (niːd) *vb.* I need two sheets of paper because this letter will be a long one.

never (ˈnevə) *adv.* Mary has never seen her grandmother because she lives in Japan.

new (njuː) *adj.* These shoes are new. I haven't worn them yet.

next (nekst) *adj.* Mary is nine years old. She will be ten next year.

next door (neks dɔː) *adv. phr.* John's house is next to ours, so we say that he lives next door to us.

next-door (neks dɔː) *adj.* John is our next-door neighbour. His house is next to ours.

nice (nais) *adj.* Mary is so nice. She lets me use her bicycle.

night (nait) *n.* It is always dark at night.

noise (nɔiz) *n.* The cars in the street make a lot of noise; we can't hear ourselves speak.

none (nʌn) *pron.* We were all supposed to go, but none of us wanted to.

normally (ˈnɔːməli) *adv.* We don't normally have fish for breakfast.

not (nɔt) *adv.* Mary is not my sister. She is my cousin.

nothing (ˈnʌθiŋ) *pron.* or *n.* I can't understand why she is afraid. There is nothing to be afraid of.

notice (ˈnoutis) *vb.* It is the first time I have noticed that this tree is a chestnut tree.

now (nau) *adv.* Last year I was rather thin: now I am rather fat.

o'clock (əˈklɔk) *adv.* What's the time . It is twelve o'clock.

of course (əv ˈkɔːs) *adv. phr.* Will you do it for me? Of course, I'll do it for you, so don't worry about it.

offence (əˈfens) *n.* It is an offence to cross the street when the lights are red.

offer (ˈɔfə) *vb.* John offered me a cigarette, but I told him I did not smoke.

often (ˈɔːfn/ˈɔːtən) *adv.* I see him very often, almost every day.

old (ould) *adj.* The old man has white hair and walks with a stick.

older (ˈouldə) *adj., comp.* of **old**.

on (ɔn) *prep.* There is a fly on the wall. I'll try to kill it.

(at) once (wʌns) *adv.* We went at once, without waiting.

one (wʌn) *pron.* Do you want an ice-cream? Yes, I think I'll have one.

only (ˈounli) *adv.* I need three cups but I have found only two.

on to (ˈɔntu) *prep.* The cat jumped on to the table and broke two cups.

open (ˈoupən) *vb.* The doctor told me to open my mouth so that he could see my tongue.

open (ˈoupən) *adj.* The door was open, and the dog went into the garden.

opposite (ˈɔpəzit) *prep.* We can look across the road into the fields because there is no house opposite ours.

opposite (ˈɔpəzit) *adj.* I have to cross the river to go to church because it is on the opposite side.

other (ˈʌðə) *adj.* You have this cake. I'll have the other one.

other (ˈʌðə) *pron.* I was the only one to stay. All the others had left.

our (ˈauə) *adj.* This is our new boat. We bought it yesterday.

out (ˈaut) *adv.* He was in the house but had to go out to pick some flowers.

outing (ˈautiŋ) *n.* One of our Sunday outings is to go and walk on the beach.

outside (ˈautˈsaid) *prep.* Leave your dog outside the shop; they do not allow dogs to go in.

over (ˈouvə) *adv.* The game is over now. Everybody must go back home.

overlook (ˌouvəˈluk) *vb.* The tower is so high that it overlooks the whole town.

own (oun) *vb.* We are the only ones in the village not to own a car.

own (oun) *adj.* (1) Peter longed to have a pony of his own. (2) She makes her own dresses. She does not have to buy them.

page (peidʒ) *n.* It is a long book. It has two hundred pages.

paid (peid) see **pay.**

pair (pɛə) *n.* I need a new pair of gloves.

parcel (ˈpɑːsl) *vb.*—parcelled, parcelled. I parcelled the present before sending it by post.

parcel (ˈpɑːsl) *n.* He put the shoes in a box and wrapped them up to make a nice parcel.

parcelled (ˈpɑːsld) see **parcel.**

park (pɑːk) *vb.* Before we can go to the shop we must find a place to park the car.

party ('pɑːti) *n.*—parties. For the party my mother invited all my friends.

pass (pɑːs) *vb.* Mary passes the Post Office every day on her way to school.

pass (pɑːs) *vb.* If Mary does not pass her examination, she will have to stay in the same class next year.

pay (pei) *vb.*—paid, paid. When I buy cakes I pay for them with my own money.

peck (pek) *vb.* Hens peck the ground with their beaks to find their food.

peel (piːl) *vb.* Do you want an orange? Let me peel it for you.

people ('piːpl) *n.* There were too many people at the cinema. We couldn't get in.

perhaps (pə'hæps) *adv.* If you have nothing to do, perhaps you would like to come with us.

pick (pik) *vb.* I wanted to eat an apple, so I went into the garden and picked one.

pick (up) (pik ʌp) *vb.* I saw a pencil on the floor. I picked it up and put it in my pocket.

pinch (pintʃ) *n.*—pinches. If you take some salt between your thumb and forefinger you will have a pinch of salt.

plan (plæn) *n.* We have made our plans for the whole week; we know exactly where to go and when.

play (plei) *vb.* After school I like to play ball with the other boys.

play (plei) *n.* "Hamlet" is a play by Shakespeare.

please (pliːz) *vb.* (1) Could you help me with my work, please. (2) I was pleased to hear that you could come with us.

plenty (of) ('plenti ɔv) *n.* The grocer asked me if I needed tomatoes but I told him we had plenty of them in the garden.

pocket-money (ˈpɔkitˌmʌni)) *n.* Daddy gives me pocket-money every week, so I have enough to go to the cinema and to the football match.

point (out) (pɔint aut) *vb.* I couldn't see the house, so he pointed it out with his finger.

popular (ˈpɔpjulə) *adj.* He is very popular. Everybody likes him.

possible (ˈpɔsibl) *adj.* Now throw your ball as far as possible!

post (poust) *vb.* I must rush to the Post Office to buy a stamp and post my letter.

pour (out) (pɔː aut) *vb.* The milk bottle is too heavy. Could you pour some milk out for me?

prefer (priˈfəː) *vb.* I prefer hockey to cricket, so I'll go and watch the hockey match.

prepare (priˈpɛə) *vb.* I helped Mother to prepare the lunch. When Father arrived it was ready.

president (ˈprezidənt) *n.* The President of the U.S.A. is the head of that country.

proud (of) (praud ɔv) *adj.* When John won the race his father was very proud of him.

provide (prəˈvaid) *vb.* The first day of school no-one had a pencil. The teacher provided each of us with one.

pull (pul) *vb.* Mary pushes her doll's pram, and I pull my toy car behind me.

punctual (ˈpʌŋktjŭəl) *adj.* He is never on time: he is not punctual.

purse (pəːs) *n.* Mother carries her money in a purse.

push (puʃ) *vb.* When I was not looking, John pushed me and I fell into the water.

put (put) *vb.*—put, put. Mother put my pen in her bag.

put (away) (put əˈwei) *vb.*—put, put. Before we leave school we put all our books away in our desks.

put (on) (put ɔn) *vb.*—put, put. You had better put your coat on if you want to be warm.

quayside (ˈkiːsaid) *n.* The boat will come to the quayside and we'll be able to get on board.

question (ˈkwestʃən) *n.* The teacher asked me the question: What happened in September 1939?

quickly (ˈkwikli) *adv.* He was in a hurry, so he walked quickly.

quiet (ˈkwaiət) *adj.* You make too much noise! Be quiet, please.

quite (kwait) *adv.* I am quite hungry, but not very.

race (reis) *n.* Peter and John ran a race to see who was going to arrive home first.

rain (rein) *vb.* It has certainly been raining: the street is all wet.

ran (ræn) see **run**.

rather (ˈrɑːðə) *adv.* Would you rather play tennis or hockey? I'll let you decide.

reach (riːtʃ) *vb.* The switch is too high. I cannot reach it.

read (riːd) *vb.*—read (red), read (red). My young brother cannot read. I must tell him all the stories.

ready (ˈredi) *adj.* Tell me when you are ready and I'll come and help you.

realize (ˈriəlaiz) *vb.* I did not realize what was happening because I was asleep.

really (ˈriəli) *adv.* I said I liked the present, but I didn't really like it.

receive (riˈsiːv) *vb.* I received a good mark for my work.

red (red) *adj.* Tomatoes are red when they are ripe.

relax (riˈlæks) *vb.* After work she was very tired, so she went on her bed to rest and relax.

remember (riˈmembə) *vb.* They told me that we used to have a big dog when I was a baby, but I couldn't remember.

remind (riˈmaind) *vb.* I forgot to post the letter this morning. Will you please remind me before I leave?

replied (ri'plaid) see **reply**.

reply (ri'plai) *vb.*—replied, replied. Mary sat down to reply to the letter she had received from her aunt.

report (ri'pɔːt) *vb.* Somebody reported to my father that I broke some eggs at the grocer's, and now he knows.

resort (ri'zɔːt) *n.* We found a marvellous winter resort and decided to spend our Christmas holiday there.

rest (rest) *vb.* John is very tired and he lies down on his bed to rest.

(in) **return** (ri'təːn) *adv. phr.* He let me play with his bicycle and in return I let him play with my football.

ride (raid) *n.* Every day I have a ride on my bicycle from here to the bridge and back.

right (rait) *adv.* Did you see that house right in the middle of the field?

right (rait) *adj.* The match really started at two o'clock, so you were right. That was when you said it would begin.

roar (rɔː) *vb.* Lions roar.

roll (out) (roul aut) *vb.* Mary rolled out the pastry until it was flat and thin.

room (ruːm) *n.* There are five rooms in our flat: the sitting-room, the kitchen, the bathroom, and two bedrooms.

rough (rʌf) *adj.* The sea is rough when there are big waves.

round (raund) *prep.* They were all seated round the table.

rowing ('rouiŋ) *n.* When we got out on the lake, I always let Peter do the rowing because the oars are too heavy.

rub (rʌb) *vb.*—rubbed, rubbed. The nurse rubbed my knee with some ointment.

rubbed (rʌbd) see **rub**.

rude (ruːd) *adj.* It is rude to talk at the same time as the teacher.

run (rʌn) *vb.*—ran, run. They saw the bus coming, so they started running to catch it.

run (over to) (rʌn ˈouvə tuː) *vb.*—ran, run. I must run over to our neighbour's to see them. I am late already.

rush (rʌʃ) *vb.* It was late. I had to rush to the station to catch my train.

sad (sæd) *adj.* I am sad because my dog died this morning.

safely (ˈseifli) *adv.* Their plane arrived safely without accident.

said (sed) see **say**.

salesman (ˈseilzman) *n.*—salesmen. A salesman goes from one shop to another to try to sell his product.

sang (sæŋ) see **sing**.

sat (sæt) see **sit**.

satchel (ˈsætʃəl) *n.* I carry my school-books in a satchel.

Saturday (ˈsætədi) *n.* Saturday is the last day of the week.

saw (sɔː) see **see**.

say (sei) *vb.*—said, said. I don't know what he said because I could not hear.

school (skuːl) *n.* Our school is very small: it has only fifty pupils.

score (skɔː) *vb.* Our team scored three goals. We won the match.

sea (siː) *n.* When we are at the seaside we swim in the sea.

(at) **sea** (siː) *n.* We went out with the yacht and were at sea for the whole day.

see (siː) *vb.*—saw, seen. The window is so dirty that I cannot see through it.

seem (siːm) *vb.* I looked outside. It seemed to be raining, so I took my umbrella.

seen (siːn) see **see**.

sell (sel) *vb.*—sold, sold. They sold their old house and bought a new one.

send (out) (send aut) *vb.*—sent, sent. Mother needed some soap and she sent Peter out to the chemist's.

serious (ˈsiərīəs) *adj.* John is always laughing. He is never serious.

serve (sə:v) *vb.* It never takes long at the baker's because he serves us at once.

several (ˈsevrel) *adj.* We'll spend several days by the sea, but I don't know how many.

shade (ʃeid) *n.* When it is too hot I don't like to sit in the sun. I prefer to sit in the shade because it is cooler.

shall (ʃəl) *vb. aux.*—should. To-day I (we) have stayed at home, but to-morrow I (we) shall go and see my (our) grandmother.

shape (ʃeip) *n.* Your balloon is round. Mine is long. They have different shapes.

shine (ʃain) *vb.*—shone, shone. When there are too many clouds, the sun does not shine.

shiny (ˈʃaini) *adj.* My shoes are dusty. I must polish them to make them clean and shiny again.

ship (ʃip) *n.* A steamer is a kind of ship.

shone (ʃɔn) see **shine.**

shop (ʃɔp) *n.* I need some flour, but there is no shop open on Sundays and I can't buy any.

(to go) **shopping** (ˈʃɔpiŋ) *vb. phr.* I must take a basket and some money as I am going shopping.

shopping (ˈʃɔpiŋ) *n.* Mother did her shopping and came back with lots of fruit, vegetables, cakes, etc.

shopping-list (ˈʃɔpiŋ list) *n.* Mother didn't buy any cheese because she forgot to write it down on her shopping-list.

should (ʃud) see **shall.**

shout (ʃaut) *vb.* He was so far away that I had to shout if I wanted him to hear me.

show (ʃou) *vb.*—showed, shown. He asked me to come in because he wanted to show me his new wireless.

show (ʃou) *n.* I'll stop at the cinema and ask at what time the show starts.

shown (ʃoun) see **show**.

shut (ʃʌt) *vb.*—shut, shut. Could you please shut the door? It's very cold.

sick (sik) *adj.* I have eaten too many sweets and now I feel sick.

side (said) *n.* I cross the bridge when I want to go to the other side of the river.

silly (ˈsili) *adj.* They say I am silly because I don't want to go with them.

sing (siŋ) *vb.*—sang, sung. I could not see the bird but I could hear it singing.

sit (sit) *vb.*—sat, sat. I am sitting in a chair and reading a book.

sit (down) (sit daun) *vb.*—sat, sat. Here is a chair for you. Do sit down.

sitting-room (ˈsitiŋ ru(ː)m) *n.* After dinner my parents and their friends went into the sitting-room to sit and talk.

size (saiz) *n.* This shirt is too small. Have you got one a size bigger, please?

skip (skip) *vb.*—skipped, skipped. Mary skipped while the other girls turned the rope.

skipped (skipt) see **skip**.

skyscraper (ˈskaiˌskreipə) *n.* The very high buildings in New York are called skyscrapers.

sleep (sliːp) *vb.*—slept, slept. I did not sleep well last night because my sister cried and woke me up.

slept (slept) see **sleep**.

slide (down) (slaid daun) *vb.*—slid, slid. Let us go to the chute and slide down.

slide (slaid) *n.* I'll have one last slide on the chute before I go back home.

small (smɔːl) *adj.* We had a small lunch: only two sandwiches and an apple.

smell (smel) *vb.*—smelt, smelt. The meal smells so good that I feel hungry already.

smell (smel) *n.* This perfume doesn't have a nice smell. I don't like it.

smelt (smelt) see **smell**.

smoke (smouk) *vb.* Father smokes a pipe but not cigarettes.

snow (snou) *vb.* It has been snowing for two hours. The ground is all white now.

so (sou) *adv.* There were so many nice toys that the children didn't know which to choose.

sold (sould) see **sell**.

sole (soul) *n.* I must have my shoes repaired because there are holes in my soles.

some (sʌm) *adj.* I would like some more jam, please.

some (of) (sʌm ɔv) *pron.* I thought everybody smoked cigarettes; but some of my friends don't.

sometimes (ˈsʌmtaimz) *adv.* Sometimes we eat cheese and sometimes we eat jam with our bread.

soon (suːn) *adv.* He'll be here very soon, in five minutes.

sorry (ˈsɔri) *adj.* Peter was very sorry to hear that John was ill.

sort (sɔːt) *n.* There are all sorts of beautiful flowers in the garden.

sound (saund) *vb.* It is not English that he speaks, but it sounds like it.

sound (saund) *n.* It was so quiet that not a sound was heard.

spare (spɛə) *adj.* You can come and stay with us, we have a spare room.

speak (spiːk) *vb.*—spoke, spoken. He spoke to me, but I don't know what he said. I did not understand.

speed (spiːd) *n.* The car passed at such a speed that we didn't have time to see who was in it.

spend (spend) *vb.*—spent, spent. (1) I spent three hours doing this work. (2) I went to the shop and spent all my money. I haven't a penny left.

spent (spent) see **spend**.

spit (out) (spit aut) *vb.*—spat, spat. I put the cherry into my mouth, but it was bad—so I spat it out.

splash (about) (splæʃ əˈbaut) *vb.* Ducks like to splash about in the water.

spoke (spouk) see **speak**.

spoken (ˈspoukən) see **speak**.

Spring (spriŋ) *n.* Flowers start growing in the Spring.

stagger (ˈstægə) *vb.* If you close your eyes, you can't walk properly. You stagger.

stall (stɔːl) *n.* In the cow-shed the farmer keeps his cows in stalls.

stand (stænd) *vb.*—stood, stood. A policeman stands in the middle of the street to direct the traffic.

stand (up) (stænd ʌp) *vb.*—stood, stood. I was sitting when Auntie came in. I stood up and offered her my chair.

start (staːt) *vb.* (1) We start school at nine o'clock every morning. (2) Mary started to read a book but did not finish it.

stay (stei) *vb.* I didn't come back home last night; I stayed the night with my uncle.

stick (stik) *vb.*—stuck, stuck. I just have to stick a stamp on the envelope and then I can post it.

still (stil) *adv.* I told him to go, but he is still here.

stitch (stitʃ) *n.*—stitches. The cut on my leg was so big that it needed six stitches to close it.

stood (stud) see **stand**.

stoop (stuːp) *vb.* He is so tall that he has to stoop to get into the car.

stop (stɔp) *vb.*—stopped, stopped. He stopped the car because the traffic lights were red.

stopped (stɔpt) see **stop**.

story (ˈstɔːri) *n.*—stories. For my birthday I received a book in which there are five good stories, and I have already read them.

stout (staut) *adj.* This man eats so much that he's going to become stout.

straight (away) (streit əˈwei) *adv. phr.* When we ask Peter to do something, he always does it straight away.

street (striːt) *n.* Before crossing a street one must look to be sure there is no car coming.

stretcher-trolley (ˈstretʃə ˈtrɔli) *n.* In hospitals, they push patients who are very ill on stretcher-trolleys.

strict (strikt) *adj.* The doctor is very strict. He won't allow me to eat a single piece of cake.

stroke (strouk) *vb.* John strokes the dog to show he likes him.

strong (strɔŋ) *adj.* Tie up the parcel with strong string that will not break.

stuck (stʌk) see **stick**.

subject (ˈsʌbdʒekt) *n.* I chose two new subjects at school this year: French and Geography.

such (sʌtʃ) *adj.* He took such a large piece of meat that he couldn't finish it all.

suddenly (ˈsʌdnli) *adv.* I wasn't expecting him, but suddenly he arrived.

suggest (səˈdʒest) *vb.* We didn't know what to do. John suggested that we should go to the zoo; it was a good idea.

summer (ˈsʌmə) *n.* During the summer the weather is hot.

Sunday (ˈsʌndi) *n.* We go to church every Sunday.

sung (sʌŋ) see **sing**.

suppose (səˈpouz) *vb.* We were supposed to go swimming this afternoon, but it started raining and we did not go.

sure (ʃuə) *adj.* He is not sure that he can come. He must ask his aunt first.

surprise (sə'praiz) *n.* Mother did not tell us you were supposed to come. It is a real surprise.

swam (swæm) see **swim**.

sweep (swiːp) *vb.*—swept, swept. Mary sweeps the floor with a broom.

sweet (swiːt) *adj.* Little kittens are always very sweet.

swim (swim) *vb.*—swam, swum. Peter swims like a fish.

swimmer ('swimə) *n.* They say Peter is a good swimmer because he can swim across the river.

switch (off) (switʃ ɔ(ː)f) *vb.* We don't need the light, switch it off, please.

switch (on) (switʃ ɔn) *vb.* When it gets dark we switch on the light.

swum (swʌm) see **swim**.

tail (teil) *n.* Mice have long, thin tails and rabbits have short, round ones.

take (teik) *vb.*—took, taken. (1) I take my sandwiches with me and eat them for lunch. (2) I wish Mummy could take me to the fair but she is ill in bed.

take (off) (teik ɔ(ː)f) *vb.*—took, taken. A man always takes his hat off when he enters a house.

take (out) (teik aut) *vb.*—took, taken. Peter took his present out of its box to show it to his brother.

taken ('teikən) see **take**.

talk (tɔːk) *vb.* I talked to him on the telephone yesterday.

tame (teim) *adj.* These pigeons are tame. They come and eat out of our hands.

target ('tɑːgit) *n.* At the shooting gallery, if you hit the centre of the target, you win a prize.

tea (tiː) *n.* At four o'clock, English people have their tea; they drink cups of tea and eat cakes.

team (tiːm) *n.* We have good men in our football team and we think we can win the match.

tear (tɛə) *vb.*—tore, torn. I can't wear my blue trousers because I tore them when I climbed over the fence.

term (təːm) *n.* In England a school year is divided into three terms: September to December, January to March, and April to July.

terribly (ˈterəbli) *adv.* It is raining terribly hard. We can't go out yet.

than (ðæn, ð(ə)n) *conj.* I am taller than you but you are stronger than me.

thank (θæŋk) *vb.* "Did you thank Mrs Brown when she gave you your present?" "Yes, I said: 'Thank you very much.'"

that (ðæt) *adj.*—those. I want that book over there—not the other one.

that (ðæt) *dem. pron.*—those. John is ill. That is why he is in bed.

that (ðæt) *conj.* Come nearer so that you can see it.

that (ðæt) *rel. pron.* The house that stands at the corner of the street is my uncle's.

theatre (ˈθiətə) *n.* We went to the theatre to see the new play.

their (ðɛə) *poss. adj.* John was with his sister, but Charles and Peter were with their young brother.

then (ðen) *adv.* I have to do my geography, then my biology, and then I can go.

there (ðɛə) *adv.* I can't find my sweater. I looked in my cupboard, but it wasn't there.

therefore (ˈðɛəfɔː) *adv.* I want to get up early to-morrow; therefore I shall go to bed early to-night.

these (ðiːz) *plur. of* **this.**

they're (ˈðeiə) = **they are.**

thin (θin) *adj.* This sweater is not warm enough; it is too thin.

thing (θiŋ) *n.* I can't see the thing you have in your hand. What is it?

think (θiŋk) *vb.*—thought, thought. I thought he was still there, but he had gone.

this (ðis) *adj.*—these. This boy here is my brother.

this (ðis) *pron.*—these. I am not sure if this is what you want.

those (ðouz) *plur. of* **that.**

though (ðou) *conj.* He is taller than me though he is a year younger.

thought (θɔːt) see **think.**

threw (θruː) see **throw.**

thrill (θril) *vb.* John was thrilled when he saw his birthday present. It was a watch.

throw (θrou) *vb.*—threw, thrown. One of the boys threw a ball to me but I couldn't catch it.

thrown (θroun) see **throw.**

thunderstorm (ˈθʌndəstɔːm) *n.* We expect a thunderstorm with a lot of rain, wind, lightning, and thunder.

ticket (ˈtikit) *n.* Mary needs a ticket to take the train and she will buy it at the booking office.

tidy (ˈtaidi) *adj.* John's room is very tidy; there is not a thing out of place.

tie (up) (tai ʌp) *vb.*—tied, tied. I cannot tie up my parcel because I have no string.

time (taim) *n.* (1) It is one o'clock; it is time for lunch. (2) Four times four is sixteen.

(on) **time** (taim) *adv. phr.* We won't have to wait for him, as he is always on time.

tired (ˈtaiəd) *adj.* I don't want to rest: I am not tired.

to-day (təˈdei) *adv.* or *n.* When Mary woke up this morning, she thought: "To-day is my birthday."

together (təˈgeðə) *adv.* We both want to see the film; let us go together.

to-night (təˈnait) *adv.* To-night we can stay up late because to-morrow is Saturday.

too (tuː) *adv.* (1) Mary has some money. I want some too. (2) I can't eat it all. You gave me too much.

took (tuk) see **take**.

top (tɔp) *n.* That little bird is singing at the top of the tree.

tore (tɔː) see **tear**.

torn (tɔːn) see **tear**.

traffic (ˈtræfik) *n.* This road is safe for children. There is no traffic at all.

train (trein) *n.* We have to be at the station at two o'clock to catch our train.

travel (ˈtrævl), *vb.*—travelled, travelled. My father travels a lot. He went to France twice, then to Germany, and now he is in Italy.

travelled (ˈtrævld) see **travel**.

treat (triːt) *vb.* John did not go to the hospital because the doctor said he could treat him at home.

trick (trik) *n.* At the fair, the clown did all sorts of tricks with a ball.

tried (traid) see **try**.

(to be in) **trouble** (ˈtrʌbl) *n.* Let's go and help Peter. He is in trouble.

trouble (ˈtrʌbl) *n.* Father has some trouble with the car. Let us go and see if we can help him.

true (truː) *adj.* He told me that John was at home, but it was not true; he was not there.

try (trai) *vb.*—tried, tried. I shall try if you wish, but I am sure I can't do it.

try (on) (trai ɔn) *vb.*—tried, tried. I wanted to see if the coat was big enough for me, so I tried it on.

turn (təːn) *vb.* Don't turn the page yet. I have not finished reading it.

turn (tə:n) *n.* It is your turn, John. You're supposed to go before me.

turn (away) (tə:n ə'wei) *vb.* He did not want to see the accident, so he turned his head away.

turn (round) (tə:n raund) *vb.* The policeman said we had gone too far, so we turned round and came back.

turn (to) (tə:n tu(:)) *vb.* Blue turns to green when you mix it with yellow.

uncle ('ʌŋkl) *n.* My father's brother is my uncle.

under ('ʌndə) *prep.* I put it under my book to hide it.

unload ('ʌn'loud) *vb.* When we came back from the seaside, we had to unload the car and carry all our things into the house.

untidy (ʌn'taidi) *adj.* Untidy people always leave things lying about.

until (ən'til/ʌn'til) *conj.* We promised to wait for him. We must stay here until he comes back.

unwrap ('ʌn'ræp) *vb.*—unwrapped, unwrapped. There was blue paper round my present. I had to unwrap it to find out what it was.

unwrapped ('ʌn'ræpt) see **unwrap**.

usual ('ju:ʒuəl) *adj.* One o'clock is the usual time for lunch.

usually ('ju:ʒuəli) *adv.* He is usually there on Saturdays, but to-day he is not.

vegetable ('vedʒitəbl) *n.* Carrots, cauliflowers, and cabbages are vegetables.

very ('veri) *adv.* I shall buy this book because I like it very much.

visit ('vizit) *vb.* I shall go and visit my friend at the hospital.

visit ('vizit) *n.* We had a visit from my uncle. He stayed with us for dinner.

voice (vɔis) *n.* He can't speak. He has lost his voice because he has been shouting so much.

wag (wæg) *vb.*—wagged, wagged. When a dog wants to show that it is happy, it wags its tail.

wagged (wægd) see **wag**.

wait (weit) *vb.* John was not ready, and I had to wait ten minutes.

wait (for) (weit fɔː) *vb.* I have been waiting for Mary for fifteen minutes, and she is not here yet.

walk (wɔːk) *vb.* My bicycle is broken; I shall have to walk.

walk (down) (wɔːk daun) *vb.* We have to walk down a hill to go to the sea.

walk (wɔːk) *n.* On Sundays Father takes a walk round the park with the dog.

wander (off) ('wɔndə ɔ(ː)f) *vb.* We can't find Peter. He wandered off this morning and has not come back.

want (wɔnt) *vb.* I am going to the park. I will ask Peter if he wants to come with me.

was (wɔz) see **be**.

wash (wɔʃ) *vb.* My hands are dirty; I must wash them before dinner.

waste (weist) *vb.* John is lazy. He never works. He wastes his time doing nothing.

watch (wɔtʃ) *vb.* When it rains we watch television.

water ('wɔːtə) *vb.* John fills the watering-can to water the carrots because the soil is dry.

water ('wɔːtə) *n.* Sea water is salty.

wave (weiv) *n.* The wind makes the waves on the river.

way (wei) *n.* We meet him every morning on our way to school.

wear (wɛə) *vb.*—wore, worn. (1) I shall wear my blue dress at the party. (2) These gloves have worn well. They still look new after two years.

weather ('weðə) *n.* The weather has been bad during the summer. It has rained most of the time.

we'd (wiːd) = **we had—we would**.

weed (wiːd) *vb.* When we weed the vegetable bed we must be careful to pull out only the grass and not the vegetables.

week (wiːk) *n.* The days of the week are: Sunday, Monday, Tuesday, Wednesday, Thursday, Friday, and Saturday.

well (wel) *adv.* He plays the piano very well. I like to listen to him.

we'll (wiəl) = **we shall.**

went (went) see **go.**

were (wəː) see **be.**

weren't (wəːnt) = **were not.**

wet (wet) *adj.* Peter fell into the water. When he climbed out all his clothes were wet.

we've (wiːv) = **we have.**

what (wɔt) *pron.* I should like to know what is in this box.

when (wen) *conj.* Do come when you are ready.

whenever (wenˈevə) *adv.* You may come whenever you like.

where (wɛə) *adv.* They couldn't find me. They didn't know where I was.

which (witʃ) *pron.* I have two books here. Which is yours?

while (wail) *conj.* After dinner, Mother and I did the dishes. While she was washing up, I dried them with a towel.

while (wail) *n.* I waited for a while. Then I decided to go.

whip (hwip) *vb.*—whipped, whipped. Mother uses her electric mixer to whip the cream before she puts it on the cake.

whipped (hwipt) see **whip.**

white (wait) *adj.* Our teeth are white.

who (huː) *pron.* I saw him for the first time and I asked him: "Who are you?"

whole (houl) *adj.* We stayed there for seven days—a whole week.

why (wai) *adv.* I don't know why she does not want to come.

will (wil) *vb. aux.*—would. To-day Mother would not let us go to the circus. I wonder if she will to-morrow.

win (win) *vb.*—won, won. I won a prize because I was first in the race.

wing (wiŋ) *n.* Birds use their wings to fly.

wish (wiʃ) *vb.* (1) We wished that we could have had a longer holiday. (2) Before I went to bed I wished her good night.

with (wið) *prep.* I like to play with my brothers.

without (wiˈðaut) *prep.* If I go out without my rubber boots when it rains, my feet get wet.

won (wʌn) see **win**.

wonder (ˈwʌndə) *vb.* We are late again. I wonder what the master will say.

(no) **wonder** (ˈwʌndə) *n.* It is so hot to-day, no wonder he wants to go swimming.

won't (wount) = **will not**.

wood (wud) *n.* Planks are made of wood.

wore (wɔː) see **wear**.

work (wəːk) *n.* I did all my work before supper so that I could play afterwards.

workroom (ˈwəːkrum) *n.* The tailor does all his work—the cutting and sewing—in the workroom.

worn (wɔːn) see **wear**.

worried (ˈwʌrid) see **worry**.

worry (ˈwʌri) *vb.*—worried, worried. Don't worry about the weather. We'll go even if it rains.

would (wud) see **will**.

write (rait) *vb.*—wrote, written. I took my pen and wrote my name on my exercise book.

written (ˈritn) see **write**.

wrong (rɔŋ) *adj.* (1) He took the wrong watch: he took mine instead of his. (2) Mary was crying. I asked her what was wrong with her, but she didn't want to tell me.

wrote (rout) see **write**.

yacht (jɔt) *n.* We have a new yacht. It is big enough to go out to sea.

yard (jɑːd) *n.* The school yard is behind the school. That's where we play when the weather is fine.

year (jəː) *n.* There are twelve months in a year.

yet (jet) *adv.* We must wait for him. He is not ready yet.

you'd (juːd) = **you would.**

you'll (juəl) = **you will.**

young (jʌŋ) *adj.* When we were very young we had to go to bed at six o'clock every night.

your (jɔː) *adj.* Let's change places. I will take your seat and you will take mine.

you're (juə) = **you are.**

yourself (jɔːˈself) *pron.* I'm sorry that I haven't time to help you repair the bicycle. You must do it yourself.

you've (juːv) = **you have.**